A SLOW DEATH

or,
The Silence of the Old World

Alexander J. Ford

Jack R. Parnell

PRAV
PUBLISHING

2024

PRAV Publishing
www.pravpublishing.com
prav@pravpublishing.com

Cover images:
Overlay drawing by Alexander J. Ford of a bas relief
from Karl Friedrich Schinkel's Bauakademie
(1836, damaged in 1945, demolished in 1962),
image preserved in Carl Friedrich Schinkel, *Sammlung Architektonischer Entwürfe*
(Berlin: Verlag von Ernst & Korn, 1858).

Images on p. 4:

Aries, the Ram and *Scorpio, the Scorpion* from William Tyler Olcott,
Star Lore of All Ages
(New York/London: G.P. Putnam's Sons, 1911).

ISBN 978-1-952671-36-4 (Paperback)
ISBN 978-1-952671-37-1 (Ebook)

DIS MANIBVS

A.C. FITZHUGH
b. 1991, d. 2018

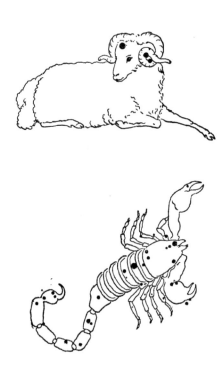

TABLE OF CONTENTS

A SLOW DEATH

or,

The Silence of the Old World

Foreword

It should be stated that we mean to avoid the manner of speaking academically, of taking the great and often misguided pains to couch each and every tiny claim in the pedantic remarks of secondary, and tertiary sources — which, as it happens, belong to bureaucrats posing as scholars more often than to proper scholars. We are not only content to indulge the prose of insular mania, for it was in such a crucible that the raw materials of these ideas were first alloyed, but beyond, we recognize that such writing possesses by nature a tempering quality that is conspicuously absent in the industry of modern academia. To disarm the work of that quality in the interest of making it more amenable to the *Alexandrian* proclivities of those who lodge themselves in the business of education, would be to disfigure it beyond repair.

The work that follows rests on two premises, which we take to be self-evident. In order to maintain a clarity of focus in the present volume, then, and to avoid getting lost in the tall grasses of terminology and of argumentation — which can so easily become irrelevant to the discussion at hand — we briefly present these premises up front, and thereafter leave such things in the lurch so as to make a proper run on the horizon.

The first being that the principles upon which Western civility has long rested are largely *foreign* to the majority of its present peoples. And the second being that the high culture for which those principles are foundational is now, and has been for quite some time, entirely decadent.

We are not the first to observe the truth of these claims in a scholarly environment. Far from it. A great deal of work already exists in the corpus of many writers to the effect of illustrating the minutiae of cultural corrosion. Our intent is more holistic. We mean to identify the essential aspects of the involutionary tendency *itself*, as its industrial regalia is presently being overhung and completed with a digital stole. With this book we mean to interrogate the epistemological mechanisms that render the involutionary tendency so continuously *appealing* to modern sensibilities.

No matter how far he may be from the city walls, the average person today can hardly help but become a bit of a metropolitan himself. So, because the work at hand requires the reader to accept as foregone certain conclusions, which are nothing if not bitter and mystical to metropolitan consideration, the question of *profit* arises. Across history this question has trailed the ascetic, darkened his eyes and rounded his shoulders. Those who are willing to labor on principle above all else grow hunched under the weight of it — the same weight that disfigures all artisan gods. Who is this book even for?

There is no mythology here and so it's useless in the foundations of anything. There are no calculations here and so it's useless in the demolition of anything. We find ourselves engaged in a torment of the elements, demanding the rigor of an academy — antagonistic, as it is, to the layman — in order to present ideas which are then in turn antagonistic to academia. It abrades the modern temperament for the simple reason that disabuse requires abrasion. Our intent with this work is to *arm* him who feels dogged by something unseen, like a hagstone placed in the hand of Peredur. Its purpose is to lend form to suspicion. It functions to quiet the orderlies, and to assure the reader that his misgivings about the Kafkaesque box — which he calls home on account of a paucity of personal agency — are, in fact, well-founded, regardless of the purse-lipped protests of his well-paid therapist. This book is, to borrow the word from Nietzsche, a rhapsody, arranged to accompany the movements of him who was already dancing, alone, without it.

Is this "traditionalism?" Who can say. It hardly matters; the word is too rife and many who attire themselves with it succeed only in reducing the idea to an issue of modern aesthetics anyhow. What we describe is no City of Ezekiel, but only the inclination to laugh in the faces of those who would. It defies terminology, that great siege-weapon of all degeneracy — useless without a metropolis against which to unleash it. Is it humanism? Nonsense. The very notion is a redress of hubris after the *fashion* of French revolutionaries. What we see, not ahead like judgement day or above like the cross of Constantine, or rather what we *observe*, not what we *envision*, is a recollection as opposed to a prophecy — not humanism, but humane in the sense that we remind man to affirm himself rather than deny himself. That living is boasting. Living is aggrandizement, prejudice, and hierarchy — only in death is there equity. Perhaps by these observations it will be argued that we mean some sort of a revolution, nonetheless — Prolix. It's an exorcism, more nearly. Only 'the people' are so cursed as to believe that the meaning of the golden age myth is in what's before us, in the future; no, futurism is incompatible with heroism. Could all this be "conservative?" Impossible, when the mentality described here constitutes nothing short of exile from the *mundus ut est*. The conservation of man, yes, but first the golems whom we've dressed up and called 'men' out of some ghastly etiquette will have to be, once again, seen through.

Reactionary? "Alright," says Cioran, "But in the same way God is."

* * *

Epigraphs

1 - José Ortega y Gasset:

"Man's real treasure is the treasure of his mistakes, piled up stone by stone through thousands of years. ... Breaking continuity with the past, warranting to begin again, is a lowering of man and a plagiarism of the orangutan. It was a Frenchman, Dupont-White, who around 1860 had the courage to exclaim: 'Continuity is one of the rights of man; it is an homage of everything that distinguishes him from beast.'"

2 - Walter Benjamin:

"This is how one pictures the angel of history. His face is turned toward the past. ... A storm is blowing in from paradise ... the storm irresistibly propels him into the future to which his back is turned, while the pile of debris before him grows skyward. This storm is what we call progress."

3 - Emil Cioran:

Whether we consider the individual or humanity as a whole, we must not identify to advance with to progress, unless we admit that going toward death is progress.

4 - Nicolás Gómez Dávila:

>*"Unable to achieve what it desires, "progress" christens what it achieves desire."*

5 - Edmund Burke:

>*"All the pleasing illusions, which made power gentle, and obedience liberal, which harmonized the different shades of life ... are to be rudely dissolved by this new conquering empire of light and reason."*

6 - R. A. Schwaller de Lubicz:

>*"The lack of philosophic foundations has given rise to [the] analytical spirit ... [our] Western scientific thinking has some obvious reasons to refuse the search for causes: The purely cerebral means at its disposal do not allow it. Besides, entering the domain of the "why" of things would have been a matter of small importance to our scientists up to now, as their faith has been staunchly materialistic and mechanistic. Their interest was entirely absorbed by the material sequence of phenomena."*

7 - Vladimir Lenin:

>*"We must organize a systematic study of the Hegelian Dialectic from a materialistic standpoint."*

8 - Renaud Camus:

>*"The non-existence of races, like the non-existence of classes, is indispensable for the industrial production of l'homie remplacable: replaceable man; exchangeable man, decultivated, decivilized, denationalized, and unrooted, such as needed by and for generalized exchange: of man with man, of man with woman, of people with people, of*

animals with things, of man with machines, with prosthesis and with objects—the post-human condition."

9 - Julius Evola:

"There is no longer breath, nor liberty, nor light, in the realm of matter, of gold, of the machine, and of number."

10 - Alexander Dugin:

"In order to fight an enemy it is first and foremost necessary to understand him, and to not succumb to his hypnosis and propaganda ... Postmodernists and the advocates of speculative realism are good in that they openly declare their intentions. Deleuze called for turning the human being into a schizophrenic (schizomass) ... and object oriented ontologists call for abolishing the human being altogether and finally extinguishing even the residually smoldering subjectivity in man to make way for the triumph of artificial intelligence, neural networks, cyborgs, or some kind of deep ecology."

11 - Lecture attendee, addressing György Lukács:

"Ah! That Hegel fellow! He should be hanged!"

12 - René Guénon:

"True ideas do not change or develop, but remain as they are in the timeless present."

13 - Emil Cioran:

"I like only vital, organic truths, the offspring of our anxiety. Those whose thoughts are alive are always right; there are no arguments against them. And even if there were, they would not last long."

14 - Arthur Schopenhauer:

> "So far, however, is reason from being the source of morality that it is reason alone which makes us capable of being rascals, which the lower animals cannot be. It is reason which enables us to form an evil resolution and to keep it when the provocation to evil is removed ... Thus Goethe said that a man may use his reason only for the purpose of being more bestial than any beast."

15 - Johann Wolfgang von Goethe:

> "Grey, dear friend, is all theory
> And green, the golden tree of life."

16 - Yehuda Safran:

> "A young boy goes off to war with a stick in hand and dreams he'll come home with a soldier's baton. Instead, he returns with a wooden leg."

17 - Ludwig Wittgenstein:

> "Anything your reader can do for himself, leave for him."

* * *

I.

PREMEDITATED CRIMES

Modernism

Wandering the American city is a miserable, stupefying experience. In Europe, much the same, albeit differentiated by the uneasy sense that the War was necessary to provide the empty real estate. Rome went up in the conflagration, and in the ashes Nero discovered the vacant land required to construct himself a palace. How fortuitous. So it was with the momentum gained by Corbusier and the Athens Charter after the War. We drift disoriented and slovenly through witless, inland seas of cheaply-made, over-engineered, and impermanent structures that could just as easily have been perpetrated on one side of the Atlantic as on the other. In our larval *ecumenopolis*, art no longer speaks for itself, but rather requires the artist to speak on its behalf. Our architecture is no different. Our literature is a mirror, rather than a portal. It reflects us in our hapless environment, and nothing more. In it, we see only a half-lidded expression, indicative of the pointless exhaustion which we sometimes occasion to hope isn't so outwardly obvious. The poetry we guiltily enjoy, knowing full-well poetry has no place in the factory, is only *bad prose*. Our work is every day stripped into increasingly specialized tasks that have no holistic character, to the point where the suggestion of holism appears like the terrifying shadow of inscrutable and tyrannical intentions. Each of these circumstances is a result of some other. Our values in our art, our art in our work, our work in our lives. The language we use to mince each other's words is now as useless-by-design as Orwell feared, the city in which we are surveilled is now as transparent and mathematized as Zamyatin feared. Even our slatternly idea of dress proceeds according to the disgust of Loos. It seems as if the simple task of finding the right words to scratch a pasquinade into the glass has become an effort of Herculean alacrity. Why?

There is a confusion of terms, centuries-thick, hanging in the air all around the question, like fog on the trenches. Modernists, Postmodernists, "Metamodernists;" Constructivists, Deconstructivists, Critical Theorists, Marxists, Neomarxists, Leninists — not Stalinists; Conservatives who conserve nothing, Liberals who despise liberty, not this but rather that; schemers, swindlers, charlatans, smoke-makers, salesmen, ad-men, marketers. Democratically elected representatives. A hundred years ago, Julius Evola wrote, "To all this let it be said, 'Enough!'"

In what soil does the root of such an enormous, strangling bramble actually lie? The simple fact — so easy to sense but so difficult to lay hold of — is that despite the mess of novel terms, all refer in one way or another to the activities of those of a sort who profess *total positivism*. So long as one makes use of their terminology, one will never be able to press them down firmly enough to demonstrate as much. Their object is obfuscation, not communication. This sort means to replace definition with something mutable; something ever-changing — and in so-doing, fortify their position. Justifying the position is, for them, of little or peripheral concern.

Definition opposes this *sort*, like the bolt in the sky over Babel; to define is to exclude. To define is to establish a line of rationale which states 'this far, and no further.' Definition, then, is a form of regulation on the scope of their fortifications. That is why the intelligentsia is so obsessed with constant, petty re-calibrations of definition. For this reason, too, are institutional academics and bureaucrat-types so appalled at anyone who presumes to speak with a convicted tone. The dialectic — that is, let us say for the moment, the inclination to fight hemming with hawing (more in due course) — requires all definitions to be partial. It requires that one's ability to grasp what Wittgenstein called 'that which is the case' only ever comes metered out in degrees.

With a constant stream of shifting terms, then, this *sort* goes about cheapening the language — no longer useful in sussing out what is consistent between individuals, the language is turned instead toward the task of putting up mutability in the dress of definitiveness. Anti-essentialism is the inevitable result: Nothing is fundamental to anything. Inalienable quality is for them prejudice by another name. Therefore, things are as man makes them to be, and man can change his mind about them at any given moment. Man imposes himself on the world, the world does not impose itself on man. That is the essential hubris of the engineer.

All across history there can be found versions of the same tradition, that of a house built to reach or rival heaven, which is made possible by the dissolution of all peoples into one single people and one single tongue. Five years prior to pulling his car to a stop at an abandoned intersection, unwrapping a razor blade, and opening his wrists and his throat, Jack Thayer privately published a short recollection of the events that unfolded the night he survived the sinking of the *RMS Titanic*. Criss-crossing the Atlantic and connecting the new world to the old world, those colossal machines reveal to the sober eye the destiny of industry: Not only failure, but more importantly, *incredulity* in the presence of failure. They were, in that day, the indisputable symbol of positivism. It was famously said that God himself could not sink the *Titanic*. Thayer described the sound of thousands of voices floundering in the frigid sea, crying out for help in pitch blackness after the ship vanished beneath them — saying it sounded like the monotonous din of a swarm of "locusts." Perhaps that sound was similar to the confusion of tongues in Genesis. Of the way of things before, he wrote:

> Nothing was revealed in the morning the trend of which was not known the night before. ... There was peace and the world had an even tenor to its ways... In those days one could freely circulate around the world, in both a physical and an economic sense, and definitely plan for the future, unhampered by class, nationality, or government... It seems to me that the disaster about to occur was the event that not only made the world rub its eyes and awake but woke it with a start keeping it moving at a rapidly accelerating pace ever since with less and less peace, satisfaction and happiness. Today the individual has to be content with rapidity of motion, nervous emotion, and economic insecurity. To my mind the world of today awoke April 15th, 1912.

Exhaustion is the consequence of acceleration. When the Gothic eye fell across Latium, the Roman writer Salvian described the weariness that suffused the Roman spirit in its death throes, saying that a fatal somnolence reigned everywhere. Though the lure to sleep is the same, in essence, from one anodyne imperial body to another, one must understand that it will always appear clothed after the timely fashion of its particular age. Beneath the clothes is the same attitude; materialism, positivism, only the costume changes — only the manner of its expression. Its present costume in the West is undergoing a transformation from industrial to digital. Léon Krier has remarked on the clever trenchancy of calling our present attempt to build Babel "modern," so to speak, as if such a thing had never occurred to man before. That the lynchpin appears now to hang in the area of language *itself* is an essential observation of this book, but before we interrogate the linguistic motor of the modern machine, as it turns today, perhaps we ought to take more clear stock of our surroundings.

Early on, man-after-industry delightfully referred to himself as "modern." The term satisfied a certain youthful vanity in the nescient, secular mind. He alone in the stream of time, armed with his mechanisms and disabused of any notion that couldn't be shown when he demanded to see it, was capable of engineering virtue for himself. Surely, whatever was good could be proved as such with sterile instruments. Qualitative reasoning; poetry, metaphysics, analogy, symbolism — these things, for the modern, constituted tyranny. They were only manacles closed around the hands of an illiterate serf by his literate slavers. It was impossible for him to foresee a corresponding tyranny of quantitative structure, like the one under the cameras of which, and ever-nearer to the microphones of which, we now write. No, his liberty was characterized by quantification. What better term to dogmatically tie the implicit, utopian tilt to that fashion than "modern." Present, now, as opposed to all-else before, then. History was no longer to be viewed as a cyclical repetition of the same lessons, known by the old and unknown to the young, taught and passed on, but rather was to be a linear thing, a vector of regressive direction and progressive direction.

The term "modern" has since been used, abused, and even now, has been somewhat discarded by the fast-moving *sort* — so concerned with their branding. Nevertheless, encoded in the fascination with presenting themselves, and their lifeless 'work,' as new today and newer tomorrow, there is the odd irony that modern man defined himself as "new" in much the same way, by naming his decadent taste modern in the first place. In other words, he can call himself novel until he runs out of air, but the impulse that drives him to do so is of course anything but. Elsewhere we called this sort the "courtiers of the new" for that very reason, though it hardly helps to continue heaping more terminology atop the mess. The decadent impulse, in its post-industrial form — the tendency toward involution — can simply be called what it has always been: *Modern*.

Modernism for our purposes can be reduced to two generations: the one being those who situate their revolutionary impulse to destroy the corrupt hierarchy in positivistic idealism, and the subsequent being those who are left to live in the culturally devastated environment prepared by the first.

For the first generation of moderns after industry, the idea was that a scientific morality could be asserted and proven. Philosophy was somehow to be put to bed in that way. The iconoclasm of these early modernists was incidental to the project of creating the perfect tradition — that is, one raised on calculated, quantifiable axioms. Dogmatic attempts to count up the uncountable — take, for instance, the 'historical materialism' of Marx — are native to that barren land. In them was awoken a Promethean stupidity, an inquisitorial will-to-destruction which, when and wheresoever it arises, is unrivaled in history by any spear-bristling horde or force of titanity. It is the idea that any man with a bible in his bag can go on and become the Pope. It isn't true. Nevertheless, the path had to be cleared of metaphysical obstacles for the rational work to proceed.

Mathematical morality was, for this first generation, the progressive eschaton. Because the project mandated so much cultural demolition to rid the hardware of 'bad' software, the first generation failed to initiate their sons with respect to anything. To them they left disassembled tools and fallow ground; they turned the livestock loose and set fire to the house, taught them nothing about the stars or the seasons, and said, 'Now you're free to go and do what you will.' But freeing them from the fields did not remove from them the capacity to starve, as it were, any more than would removing a man's feet give him no reason to be anywhere else. So the next generation of moderns was exposed to the elements, and to hunger.

The second generation of moderns contended with the absurdity of the position into which they were born, as if with their own damnation. Abandoned in the industrial wilderness with their symbolic faculty stripped from them by force, and by design, they surrendered quickly to lassitude. No matter how hard they tried, and still try, to find footing in a world of complete dialectical relativity, one synthesis inevitably decays into the next thesis. Primeval hypocrites, they attack themselves, the critical eye of the intellect transfixed at last on itself, like a cancer. The very notion of the Wittgensteinian *case* became only a setup for another smug sophist to wag his finger, and hold out his own collection tin. Iconoclasm was no longer incidental to the project of counting right-behavior, it was the project. Iconoclasm for its own sake. So the artist set aside the brush and began his affair with the exegesis.

Postmodernism was not a progressive development of modernism; it came in-tow with it like blood from a wound. It didn't take long under such circumstances for the academic enterprise to slough off and leave behind only the bones of business, with lecturers-for-hire antithesizing each other's products as soon as they came on the market. As they say in academia, publication is lifeblood. Hence, speaking with most intellectuals today feels hardly different from speaking with salesmen. Plato, of course, warned us of this in the *Gorgias*, but enough of the particulars. There's money to be made; the show must go on and we play two shows a night.

To say it simply, then, the first decadents are those people who pathologically take apart what they've been given for the "greater good," and the second are those who have been given nothing, and so call "good" whatever prolongs their useless existence. Or rather, the second believe that the moral is an illusion, an oppressive wool pulled over the eyes of the venerable low-borns by the villainous aristocrats; and so they call anything that allows for their continued, worthless *subsistence* "progress," implying "good" without having to blaspheme by saying what they mean, without having to appeal to prejudice in the form of hierarchy. There is no third generation. By nature, the second perpetually reclothes, redefines, and reimagines itself at the individual level until it is either conquered by an unwearied people, or assimilated into one. Either way, dissolution into the dream of history is the result.

It is a strange irony that the centuries-old materialist position — the existence of an 'objective reality,' beyond sense data — inevitably transformed into the dogmatic relativity of truth. The idea is no longer that a scientific formulation will come along, be proven, and yield a utopian set of predications. Only the most naive and poorly-read modern still clings to the hope that some person or policy will one day deliver them from each other. Now the idea is even more perverse: that because language cannot make meaning, its purpose is to consolidate power. Power *names* the object of its desire utopian. So the truth itself is antithesized at last, re-characterized to be whatever it is the party requires it to be, while the intelligentsia argue among themselves about the meaning of the word. The dialectical process assumes the role of truthfulness. What is "true" is only the gradient of perspectival falsehood left by the dialectic.

A caricatured priest, of the sort who so terrifies the democratic voter, interprets the scriptures for his illiterate mass according to the designs of the bureaucrats who employ him. How terrible, yes, yes. And yet, all around us, the so-called 'expert' interprets the data for his own mass, according to the design of the bureaucrats who employ *him*, just the same. The dialectic is the thing which keeps these secular, educated layman "illiterate," after the same fashion as his medieval counterpart. This state of affairs is only assured if one accepts the premise that language is a complete system for the apprehension of reality. For the man of antiquity, that notion was roundly rejected. For us however, not so much. Knowingly, or unknowingly, all forms of modern secularism *rest* on that premise. The opposing position is that language only approximates reality, that metaphysical imperatives cannot be wholly reduced to linguistic entrapment, and therefore, that what is true exists regardless of whether or not the rhetoric can accurately encapsulate it.

Julius Evola remarked that "The idea of progress...is a Western superstition which has arisen from the Jacobin ideology." For a moment we will set aside the question of origin.

According to the superstition, there exists some industrious predisposition, as if an evolutionary force, which — unless interfered with by nefarious actors — retains only what is good and leaves what is bad. There is a cold, automatic efficiency that directs the alleged progressive mechanism, irrespective of we worthless individuals caught up in the flow of its benevolent, and indifferent motion. To look away is to deprive us all of technology, to *mortalize* us, and to subject us all to discomfort. The modern looks upon the cynic as if he means to take the food out of his mouth, and the pillow out from under his head. To fight the current for any reason is a dangerous charade of selfishness, for which one is to be shaken by his shoulders for his own good, but more importantly, for the sanctimonious good of someone else.

Politicians, professors, 'experts,' and activists lecture us day-in and day-out: Man's purpose is to facilitate progress. Progress is measurable, material, and can be offered as a sufficient answer to the question of virtue.

Those things we call modern in architecture or in the arts are demonstrably regressive, and yet are pawned off as if they are somehow quantifiably progressive—as though the humanities are a matter of computation and solution. Every day another permutation of the same appellate progressivism sends up new shoots in the academic loam. Tenured types cannot agree on the precise moment when the modernist first arrived on the scene, nor the moment when the curtain allegedly fell on the whole carnival, though they do all seem to agree that whatever is happening now is surely some sort of intellectual frontier — one beyond modernism. Like the mercantile pressure to continuously produce a growth in profits, the moderns are engaged in the production of evermore progressive terminology.

For a mentality that relies entirely on the appeal to novelty and individuality — "progress," these old things are now called — to confront one's dependence on, and constant recitation of now century-old maxims is likely some sort of ego death. A certain air of vapidity typifies the world around us, today, in the West. Though it's often said of age that it carries with it wisdom, like a sweet scent on a fair wind, seldom is it offered in the same breath that there is age still beyond wisdom, and in those endmost years there is nothing but fragility, senility, and collapse. So Cioran remarked that just as a flower is not complete until it's fallen, the same may be said of a civilization.

* * *

Revolution

It is not the various activities of demise, but rather the coming of the will-to-fall *itself* — hoisted like heraldry by the figures who precipitate the end — with which we are concerned. Not corruption, but corruptive potential. The will-to-fall is refined in all metropolitan environs. It belongs to the places, people, and institutions that allow for idealists to cultivate their intellectual weeds untried by the natural fires that test a man's constitution beyond the city walls. The same involution in thought faced Lycurgus and Napoleon; it faces us now. And so, we observe that the progressive superstition — as Evola termed the will-to-fall, and as we know it today — originated with the French revolutionaries. It approaches us through modern history therefrom. By the nineteenth century, Marx and Marxist theorists looked with eagerness toward the French example. It's no elusive thing that materialistic progress is a central conceit of Marxist mythology. In fact, an early communist disposition is visible even in the ideas of the Diggers and Levellers of late-Medieval England. Marx himself noted that the French arranged the foundations for communism upon an even older, reactionary English naïveté. So John, King of England, scowled.

The educated eye will perhaps be drawn away from the discussion of modernism at hand, recognizing something similar to the dialectic advanced by Hegel (transmuted into a kind-of mathematical eschatology by Marx) even on the tongues of ancient intellectuals in Athens. Hegel himself noted Socrates' apparent use of the dialectic. That idea was ingeniously described in Nietzsche's *Birth of Tragedy*, there named "Socratism," for Nietzsche identified Socrates as the progenitor of the strange subjugation of the activities of the arts to the terminology of the sciences; of the ritual to the doctrinal. It's common knowledge that Socrates was accused of corrupting the Athenian youth, but few understand what is actually meant by the accusation, preferring instead to scoff as though the fate which befell him was identical to that which befell Galileo.

We might remark here as well, in passing, that the medieval issue of universals, which arose from a text translated to English by Boethius — originally written by Porphyry — the "Isagogue" to Aristotle's *Categories*, touches on a similar dialectical issue. Ironically, or perhaps prophetically, throughout history some reductive, anti-metaphysical force, going by different names, haunts the marketplace as a creature of recurrence. It appears time and again to stalk the streets of cities set upon by moral or cultural decay from Sodom to Berlin. We are reminded of a brilliant remark made by Bossuet, that it was Cain who created the first city, in order to have a place in which to elude his remorse. To trace the complete history of the will-to-fall in all its forms would exhaust an entire generation of scholars. Our concern is only with its modern expressions, and so we train our eye on the French. As we see, the Jacobins deployed appeals to political progress, as a matter of scientific suasion, in order to justify the messy process of replacing the power of the clergy over the state with the power of the new revolutionary party.

In the summer of 1790, the *Constitution civile du clergé* was passed into law, which effectively brought the Church entirely beneath the new government. The general programme of "Dechristianization" which was advanced, piecemeal, by the revolutionaries included, in addition to the seizure of all Church lands by the state, the desecration of statues and iconography, the destruction of bells or other public signs of worship, the legalization of divorce, and the criminalization of monastic vows. Countless public, often torturous executions were carried out absent any semblance of just process throughout the 1790s. Judgement was frequently summary, and administered by mob.

Of course a certain portion of the French peasantry did sympathize with the revolutionary position that both the Church and the old state apparatuses were then financially decadent, irredeemably corrupt, and oppressive institutions. However, many modern historians who are adamant to lionize the whole affair, for the simple reason that the French Revolution is the mother of our modern disposition in the West, pay little heed to the fact that the peasantry was quite far from united on the specific issue of the Church. In other words, dissatisfaction with the bureaucracy of the institution — with what Evola called "hypocritical religiosity" — was not at all the same as dissatisfaction with Christian ideals, Christian metaphysics. A reverent look at the genocide in the Vendée more than demonstrates that fact.

Then, the need to keep the mask of the Church at least somewhat affixed to the face of the polity remained, for as we see in the Vendée, the mentality of agrestal France was not yet wholly secularized. Thus can we make sense of seemingly contradictory actions of the revolutionaries: they executed nuns and turned their cannonfire on cathedrals one day, and yet the next, took special care to replace priests in conservative dioceses with puppets who were loyal to the new government, all to maintain the image of a functional mass.

Edmund Burke observed the progressive tilt of the French Society of Revolutionaries, when he described the "double fraud" of "improving" liberty as a matter of international fashion. The strange notion that liberty might be improved, even in Burke's day, establishes just how old these modern ideas are. For the Jacobins it was a clear and existential concern to render the power of the Church subservient to the power of the party, as complete abolition of spirituality, that is, total secularization of the working class, obviously proved impossible.

At first glance, it appears that the gentlemen of the Society for Revolution were faced with the task of supplanting the crown, which was divinely ordained. They would need to advance, then, a material proof to replace that appeal to divinity. And yet, Burke points out that the appeal to divinity was, already by his time, largely anachronistic. Rather, it was a matter of common understanding that the hereditary succession of the crown was a principle of secular worth.

"The people of England," says Burke, "Look to the hereditary succession of the crown as among their rights, not their wrongs; as a benefit, not a grievance; as a security for their liberty, not as a badge of servitude... They conceive of the undisturbed succession of the crown to be a pledge of the stability and perpetuity of all other members of our constitution." The idea that monarchical governance is always and exclusively raised atop a foundation of spiritual tyranny is a deeply modern misapprehension. And so, Burke goes on to describe the practice of democracy as bandied around by the revolutionaries, and as emulated by the young Americans of that day, as in essence a system of endless *coup d'état*. Every four years there is a hostile takeover of the apparatus of governance, and what lunacy we buy in the facade of collective control (a glamorous phrase, but a contradiction in practice) comes at the expense of sovereignty, stability, and perpetuity.

Already we see the French revolutionaries leaning toward the progressive superstition, which Burke called *improving liberty*. That tilt would emerge matured under the mechanized guise of "progress" in relatively short order. Toward the question of the hereditary succession of the French crown — and whether or not such a policy was of divine indefeasibility — Burke points out that it would have been a far more sensible solution to predicate succession constitutionally, by sober legislation instead of divine appeal, than it was to throw the crown out entirely because one particular mode of its justification was simply too tied up in corrupt ecclesiastical institutions.

Similarly, few would disagree that the abolition of an institution like slavery in the West was a just and moral action to take. For we in America have enshrined life, liberty, and the pursuit of happiness; that we might call the carriage of justice "progress" is an odd thing altogether. This distinction becomes an important one, should we venture to consider the worrying new tendency in the West to deface and destroy public monuments for their role in whatever the most fashionable type of intellectual self-deprecation is on any given day.

Consider the following remark from Burke — not in the light of the crown — but rather as it applies to the statues toppling now in our own cities in the name of innumerable and crudely supposed fears, or ideologies, conjured up in the moneyed halls of our so-called educational institutions:

> These sophists substitute a fictitious cause, and feigned personages, in whose favor they suppose you engaged, whenever you defend the inheritable nature of the crown. It is common with them to dispute as if they were in conflict with some of those exploded fanatics of slavery, who formerly maintained what now I believe no creature maintains...

Prior to Revolution in France, the Church possessed the exclusive power to define the good and moral citizen. And so, it became the critical issue for the revolutionaries to position that power in the hands of the government instead. This single concern was then, and is still, the soul of all modern revolutionary agitation. It can be seen acknowledged as such in the *Declaration of the Rights of Man and the Citizen* of 1789, Article IV:

> Liberty consists of doing anything which does not harm others; thus the exercise of the natural rights of each man has only those borders which assure other members of the society the enjoyment of these same rights. These borders can only be determined by the law.

Here, a 'right' is delicately suggested to be something like the freedom to engage in any activity that does not disallow anyone else from doing that thing. Having supplied this reflexive 'definition,' which in fact defines nothing at all, which is circular, and willowy at best when subjected to scrutiny, the question inevitably follows: But what is a right? The revolutionaries are thus asked to say what it is they've longed to say the whole time: "These borders can only be determined by the law." Or, in other words, they are less concerned with defining your rights, and more concerned with making sure that the power to do so is exclusive to the state. Whatever your rights are, they are what *we* say they are, whenever we deign to say so, not *you*. In this way, the revolutionary committee did not create a just government, they did not root out corruption, they did not fix any broken thing in particular. They merely executed a simple *coup d'état*, and then immediately engaged themselves in its careful justification. Anyone in history who ever presumed to topple one man from his chair and then seat himself on it has done much the same. Looking behind the veil of good marketing, so to speak — the dialectics of power or however you prefer — there is only one issue that much matters. And that is: Does history show us that these revolutionary scaffolds aid in the construction of great works, or in the utter dismantling of them? By boasting that you can strictly define the limits of liberty, as you must if you claim to protect it by law, you must then also have total control *over* it, and therefore are free to redefine decidedly despotic ways of life as either the height of liberty, or, as *in the constant pursuit of it*. Progress, we say.

Although the ideological contraption presented here in prose is clever, no doubt, progress remains an unconvincing substitute for spirituality in a world where the layman remains pastoral, in a world where the modern industries have not yet emptied the countryside into the factories. Such conditions were not quite present in revolutionary France, but, they in fact formed the social *backbone* of political unrest in Russia hardly a hundred years later.

The Bolsheviks relied in no small part on the social discord in Russia in order to solidify their grasp on the state. That sense of civil enmity was exacerbated by the rapid industrialization of the peasantry during the reign of Tsar Nicholas II. Public perception of Nicholas at the turn of the century was poor. Viewed as weak and ineffectual, Nicholas and the Empress Alexandra Feoderovna went to great lengths to conceal the medical invalidity of their only son and heir, Alexei, who was born with a rare blood condition. For Alexei, even small bruises could prove life-threatening. Alexandra was not particularly endeared to the Russian public either. Her strange demeanor was often interpreted as arrogance and indifference. Her German birth, and the fact that she struggled to learn French — the language of the Russian court — coupled with her strong accent, caused her to be perceived acutely as a foreigner. What's more, she famously turned to the enigmatic and widely reviled mystic Rasputin, who demonstrated the inexplicable capacity to ease Alexei's pain during bouts of internal bleeding. Because Rasputin was often able to calm him, and as far as the Empress was concerned, to *alleviate* his condition, Rasputin worked his way into what the Russian public generally viewed as a de facto position in the royal court.

At that time, Rasputin maintained his own brand of religious unorthodoxy, which did not help the average Russian's disgust with Nicholas's court. Rasputin was a deviant; he was a well-known member of an orgiastic faction of spiritualists called the Khlysty. Put briefly, the Khlysty engaged in grotesque sexual rituals, holding as a central tenet the idea that one is never closer to God than at the precise moment they are blessed with forgiveness. Therefore, Khlysty would engage in the most debauched behavior in order to experience the divine bliss of the absolute deepest forgiveness.

All of this occurred more or less contemporaneously with the large-scale migration of Russian peasants from the countryside to the cities and the period of explosive industrialization that underscored Nicholas's doomed reign. The momentum of scientific materialism merged with a general sentiment that the Orthodox Church and its monarchical leaders were, as was the case during the French Revolution a century-and-a-half earlier, corrupt. The difference was, this time, that a certain technological inertia did manage to reach the critical capacity necessary to sever the traditional, spiritual chords — exemplified by the Church — that defined the national identity of the Rus'. The idea of the primacy of the scientific over the spiritual became, at long last, commonplace and enticing. It didn't help the Tsar's popularity that he had also horribly mishandled war in the East. What's more, his court and his wife appeared to be captured by the Khlysty. It is in this context that the Marxist forms of art began to appear, like weeds in an unkempt garden.

Throughout the nineteenth century, dozens of writers struggled to justify the complete unmasking of the secular state to the polity, in overture to revolution in Russia. By the time the Tsarist government was overthrown, modernity was no longer a distant theory postulated by forward thinking French aristocrats, it had already urbanized the Russian economy. Like the Abbots in France, the Orthodox Church then found its lands seized by the Bolsheviks, who in January of 1918 proclaimed the people completely rid of "religious *and* anti-religious propaganda." Must it even be said that one can be sure he's being swindled by his masters when the government declares his nation free of propaganda?

There was no facile political attempt to replace clergymen loyal to the White Russians with others amenable to the Bolshevik government, as the Jacobins did; there was no need. By 1917, the fields were emptying and the factories and cities were swelling. A purely materialistic perspective is far more amenable to such an uprooted people. As Lenin explained, "Atheism is a natural and inseparable part of Marxism, of the theory and practice of scientific socialism."

Lenin wrote to E. M. Skliansky in the fall of 1920, concerning planned actions in countries neighboring Russia, saying that his new government would "...choke by hand the bourgeoisie, the clergy and the landowners. There will be an award of 100,000 rubles for each one hanged." Russian churches were stripped of their marbles, which were then used as ornamentation for new public transportation stations. In effect, the church was deconstructed and its traditional regalia repurposed to dress the strange mannequin which the Bolsheviks propped up, and insisted was in fact Russia herself, not unlike Sporus was castrated, called a woman under penalty of death, and paraded around in the dress of Poppaea before the Romans. The coffers of the clergy were raided and symbolically "redistributed" among the public, even as they stood in bread lines with starvation around the corner. Other places of Orthodox worship were demolished and replaced with public amenities — a cathedral replaced by a public swimming pool in one infamous case. The church, and with it any semblance of the metaphysical, was amputated. In Marx and Engels, the political doctrine of progress finally found surgical hands capable of isolating it from the natural sciences and transplanting it into the social animus. The key ingredient, it seems, was the materialistic demoralization of the Russian peasant, supplied as anesthetic.

It is neither our purpose to take the side of the Church, nor to present Marx's materialistic prestidigitation in a favorable light. Quite the contrary. We are ill concerned with the Church as an institution, corrosive as it no doubt had become in France on the eve of Napoleon. Few bodies are as lame, deaf, and dumb with respect to the ongoing tragedy of modernity as is the contemporary Roman Catholic Church. Let the reformers see to their churches, and be warned against the use of protestant chisels. It does not take a man of towering erudition to recognize that, as in the time of Luther, when the Papacy took to selling degrees of salvation as a matter of business, something is desperately amiss. Similarly, it is not in our interest to ignore the lamentable state of affairs for the French peasantry prior to the revolution; local gubernatorial apparatuses, dukes and barons were largely free to act as they pleased — and human nature is a persistent thing, for better or worse. What is important to the matter at hand, however, is to understand that the role the Church played, in being a seat of a metaphysical tradition, was to strengthen the will of the people against political exploitation and intellectualized *suicide*.

The Enlightenment principles which fomented revolution in Russia did so by dint of the persuasiveness of the idea that empirical scientific inquiry would, inevitably, be able to provide a fully quantified explanation of the entire human experience. Metaphysical philosophy was supposed to be made obsolete by scientific materialism. This idea was as seductive in Marx's time as it was in Bacon's. It remains seductive today. The very word metaphysics is synonymous in the mind of the average person with a kind of psychological trickery, the medium for which is rhetorical. The Philistines who proffer this idea are still content to ignore the logical issues festering at the root of scientific materialism, content to hand-wave them away as passing curiosities of an age which they have insisted is soon-to-be bygone, for now three hundred years and counting.

We will take pause for a moment to reiterate: Religion is only the so-called 'opiate' of the masses in such a bloated and bureaucratic form as we find it hobbling around today, and in the days preceding past revolutionary moments. Surely, the reformative genius of Zarathustra was to wrestle similar institutions back from the perilous brink of good business in his own time, not to give them a shove after the fashion of Luther or Robespierre, Marx, or the satyrs who bound after him.

Unfortunately for us, religious reformation can no longer serve as a catalyst for political reformation. The Western masses have long since been brought low beneath a perverted modern dogma, which holds that by virtue of its concern with metaphysical philosophy, Religion —carefully conflated with the bureaucrats who are ever in need of a reformative cuffing —

cannot have any bearing on material reality. Those who hold this position tend to fail to fathom that by questioning the materialistic foundations of spirituality, they have already accepted the nonsensical premise that metaphysical matters are subject to the scrutiny of dialectical materialism. As we will explore further, when the state assumes complete control over the definition of a good and moral citizen, and when morality becomes a matter of democratic accord alone, then the populace is left with no shield to prevent themselves from being completely enslaved by international private interests. The positivistic or *physical* power of the state will always have greater latitude to manufacture material evidence, or to conceal, re-interpret, or destroy it. By contrast, the antagonistic or *metaphysical* power resists material characterization by its very nature, and therefore, shelters us beneath idiomatic truths that are not defined by carefully tallying numbers, or coins, or by accreting questionnaires.

* * *

Metaphysics

In the third book of Xenophon's *Memorabilia*, Socrates takes notice of a young man named Epigenes, who Plato recalls as being "in poor condition, for a young man." Socrates comments in passing that Epigenes looks as if he needs exercise, to which the young man responds, "I am not an athlete, Socrates." From here, Socrates interrogates the implication that health, strength, and good physical condition are only desirable traits in the realm of athletic competition. During his analysis of Epigenes' strange aversion to his own health, Socrates makes two points which we will supply as exemplary of the idea of the *supertechnological* matter, or if you will, of the metaphysical undertaking. The first is teleological. "For you can rest assured," Socrates says, "that there is no kind of struggle...and no undertaking in which you will be worse off by keeping your body in better fettle." The second point, beyond arguing against the frivolous assertion that good health is a matter of competitive novelty, is Socrates' final statement, that strength and good physical condition "will not come of [their] own accord."

Developing strength, health, and thereby an emergent or incidental quality in one's own body is, in essence, a ritual that one observes. This is the precise meaning of orthopraxy, or, correct practice. Moreover, as Socrates hints in the matter of fettle, there is the cultivation as well of a component of self-discipline, which is entirely beyond the purview of the natural sciences and their technologies. These qualities cannot be handed over in a lesson on the board. They cannot be transferred in the form of doctrinal awareness alone. Being told the path to strength does not make one strong. There is no mechanical or chemical process that can imbue the slovenly mind with discipline. Neither words nor technology can impart these qualities on a person. Only through ritual are they attained. The metaphysical rituals — or praxis, as we have said — that yield those fruits are inflicted upon oneself, by oneself, and each generation must re-earn, re-till and re-harvest the field of the self by their own willing expenditure.

Common among the intelligentsia today is the idea that 'metaphysics' is a term synonymous with dismissible stupidities like spiritism and alleged neopaganism. So often is the word conflated with the kitschy trappings of commodified wiccanism, which enjoy popularity among a contingent of leftist charlatans who are desperate to discover a toothless mystical *style* that's acceptable to the modern *modus vivendi*. The "metaphysical" is cast in the fashion of a reactionary term with no concrete meaning, best suited as a catch-all for superstitious quackery. On the contrary, however, metaphysics is a terribly easy thing to define, much to the irritation of the institutions. We'll do so now.

We can take the natural sciences to refer, broadly, to the oracular task of divining what will occur, through categorical study of what has already occurred. Technology, then, can be defined as those things which make more efficient, or ergonomic, the imposition of the human will onto the natural world. What is technological and what is physical are explicitly intertwined. Technology and physicality characterize one another.

Therefore the question of metaphysics is revealed: Are there tasks which cannot be made easier or more efficient by technological intervention? The inability to gain technological traction on such an issue dictates that it lies beyond the realm of *physis*. Metaphysics thus pertains to those things which cannot be affected by the application of technology.

In failing to recognize the *supertechnological* nature of the qualitative endeavors, and in characterizing the traditions which are concerned with their cultivation as only crude approximations of the knowledge awarded by positivistic interrogation, one destroys the circle of toil and supplants it with the line of progress. To reduce metaphysics via technology in this way is, simply put, to refuse initiation, to automate the process, and in so doing the goal withers away to simply lifting the stone and no longer strengthening the back.

At a glance, technological development appears to bolster the *veracity* of progressive ideology. It recasts the progressive superstition as a natural fact. Today, each new generation is, on account of the momentum of industry and its specific tools, more and more alien to the previous generation. As a result, our idea of ourselves has, of course, collapsed. We might observe that from father to son, man of antiquity faced more or less the same struggles, with more or less the same tools, and in accord with such circumstances he formulated the doctrine of cycles. By contrast, modern man faces newer and newer struggles, which are only made possible, or only made *intelligible* by newer and newer tools. He has done away with the doctrine of cycles and adopted instead a linear view of things. Whereas before, our ancestors shared recourse in the form of the sword, the world around modern man is a mutable, changing thing; the very circumstances of his existence within it are hectic, undependable, and are subject to erratic motion. The terms with which he pretends to some certainty about his surroundings are constantly shuffled. Those who went before him were as if actors on a different stage in a different production. One can hardly relate to them, and because of this, one must imagine, or must *presume* much of them.

It is important at this juncture to spare some words in describing the modern attitude that one can alter man as well as alter his environment in order to better suit one another. We cannot arrive at such an idea as a *possibility* without first subscribing to total positivism. And yet further, it's a bit more insidious than that; when we take on the total positivistic worldview, the idea that man and his surroundings can, and thus *ought*, to be reengineered to better suit one another becomes not just possible, but inevitable. The question then becomes, according to whose design? Or, if you like, according to which metric? Materialism is the original reactionary force. It calls forth positivism. Positivism, in providing technological developments that do, in fact, demonstrate 'true' progress in a quantifiable sense ('this' more measurably more efficient than 'that') in turn carries with it the progressive *superstition*. Enchanted by industrial charms and talismans, one begins to believe that things which defy material encapsulation, which cannot be subjected to engineering and improved on material grounds, are only illusory. They are responsible for the comparative hardships with which he lived before. In this way, the first generation modernist is reared: He will seek either to re-engineer or to deny the immaterial. Willing as he is to say that "only things that can be measured can be said to *be*," he must then take on board that everything which is, is subject to technological intervention, that everything does essentially lend itself to manipulation at the hands of man. Said another way, he must take it on board that all things can only be called things at all, according to their capacity to be arrayed in a quantifiable matrix. Together, these ideas make utterly unavoidable the pretension that man's duty is not to construct the temple, but rather, to construct the perfect environment — the state — and as well to populate it with the perfect inhabitants.

This, of course, is not to say that technology is the specific culprit; it's only to say that it's typically provided in bad faith as *justification* for positivistic tyranny. In fact, all achievements of high culture in the long march of history have called into being some new technology, in order to allow the artisan to "collaborate," as Eliade wrote, "in the work of the gods." The problems only begin to arise when the economy is allowed to set restrictions on the vision, rather than being held subservient to it. The architect was born for the purpose of the monument; the monument was not struck into being by some architect who was otherwise wandering around with no purpose. A hammer is a thing with which man may *either* build or destroy great works. The technology is not the great work in itself. Both a vandal and a sculptor use their hammers; both a vandal and a sculptor work their stone by subtracting from it. But one makes rubble, and the other makes a masterpiece.

The modern religion holds that Man's nature, his very nature *itself*, must change. He must either learn or be forced to desire what is undesirable: to desire himself as he already is. To him is said "The purpose of work is to be *done*." The old religion, instead, holds that Man's nature *is* to change himself. He must enter the crucible as he will, for the fire of the becoming soul and the fire of conflict are one and the same. To him is said, "The purpose of work is to *be*." So we see that the modernist is defined by a kind of technological zealotry, which contains for its central principle this conceit: that the nature of man can be forcibly altered by positivistic processes. That men, therefore, are whatever they are called. The alchemical pressure to improve himself qualitatively, or spiritually, if you will, which he feels by nature, must be done away with. Only in cutting that internal cord can man's mentality be re-woven in such a way as to benefit the project of engineering the eschaton. Such a thing, he is assured by those who should know, is desirable. It's been studied and measured. Personal conflict, then, is antithesized by machinery. In his greatest novel, Cormac McCarthy described the metaphysical nature of conflict. He wrote, "War endures because young men love it, and old men love it in them." The true spirit of that idea is lost on the cosmopolitan — like Christ with a spear in his gut, peering down his nose at the centurion and presuming to pity him. What a shame, they say in the salons, the way young men with the wrong idea become old men with the wrong idea. And yet, nevertheless, one who has been taught to hate conflict is fat, because he will not wage war on his body, is dumb, because he will not wage war on his mentality, is miserable, because to shrink from bloodshed is to shrink from happiness, and is destroyed, because he will not fight to preserve himself against another who would.

What is done is not meaningfully different from what *is*. Elsewhere we have discussed this strange and obvious idea — that *doing* and *being* are hopelessly intertwined. To say what *is* is difficult, but to say what *does* is self-evident, in the same way that we may not be able to categorically set out the meaning of culture, but we recognize its absence, and we know when we see it. Wherever there is something crafted, there too is a craftsman who *is*. When he is done he *is* no longer, and so long as the work is unfinished, then he *is*. For him, metaphysics is a form of apotropaic magic. This is why so many technologies, and technology in so many environments, is so appalling. It's why industry has ruined us as if to ruin us was its primary function. It's why modern man believes with such protestant fervor, sunken into his chair, that man is nothing. Because it shifts the object of doing away from *being*, and toward being *done*. It economizes the end of action. Men may dominate the process of doing, but being done is the dominion of the machine. The machine says, "I will do in your place," and thus what it actually intones is this: "I am, and you are no more."

* * *

Arithmetic

Marx gave his own account of the genesis of modern materialism, as he saw it, in an 1844 essay on the subject, which first appeared in a collection of writings titled *Aus dem Literarischen Nachlass von Marx und Engels*. Marx wrote: "The French endowed English materialism with *esprit* and eloquence, with flesh and blood, with temperament and grace." Explicitly in this regard, Marx concluded, "The more advanced French Communists developed ... the materialist doctrine into real humanism and the logical basis of Communism." The connection between modern revolution in France, and later in Russia, is thus affirmed by Marx to be a philosophical continuum, beginning with Enlightenment work undertaken by the French and culminating in global communism.

The central issue for those early modern intellectuals was this question: How does the human rationale interface with the material world? Revolutionary theorists and political aspirants were not, in any decadent age, ignorant of the political utility contained within the ability to provision an answer to the question of interface, which could re-define metaphysical imperatives in material terms. Such a thing would remove the oldest and most crucial limiting factor on the power of the state in any healthy imperium: its priests.

Attitudes toward the nature of the interface between the individual human rationale and the material world have for centuries been collected into two generally opposed camps.

The one might simply be called the material arguments, which hold that only what is physical is fundamental and irreducible, and so either dismiss the metaphysical as illusory, or, attempt (strongly or weakly) to reduce it to physical terms. The other are the phenomenal arguments, which suppose that both the metaphysical and the physical are each irreducible, fundamental aspects of reality. The former tends to take precedence among moderns on account of its necessary acceptance of the (troubled) principle of causal closure, that is, the assertion that all physical effects or events must have an exclusively physical cause. This idea quite clearly underwrites all scientific and thereby technological enterprises.

What's important to gather here is that, historically, the materialist positions became attached to a secular, scientific worldview, bolstered by the shared requirement for causal closure. The phenomenalist positions became attached to a religious, or 'mystical' worldview for contrary reasons. There was no victory. The weight of both industry and of political machinations eclipsed the issues implicit in the materialist position. It's generally accepted by modern consensus, or perhaps, rather, by modern fashion that anything which cannot be measured, whether by mathematical formulation, or by analytical linguistic formulation — it makes no difference — is fanciful, poetic, phenomenalist nonsense.

From antiquity it's been understood that material reality can be represented (or, even, simulated) by numbers. Positions can be represented by numbers in geometric space; complex interactions between objects can be represented by equations according to specific syntax, which render variables like position, or velocity as numeric quantities — or ratios. Simulation in this way engenders predictability. Predictability engenders knowledge of what will occur based on a numerical measurement of what has already occurred. In conducting mathematical operations, one is manipulating symbols which stand in for, or approximate, what is the case.

While most mathematicians have tended to view this principle in the sense that it suggested theirs was the truest language, a universal language through which truth was completely derivable — this being a self-evident claim only waiting patiently for someone to prove it — Kurt Gödel viewed it to suggest the opposite. With the publication of his Theorem of Incompleteness in 1931, Gödel demonstrated that there exist mathematical statements which are both true and yet *unprovable*, provided that we accept that mathematics is able to render logically true statements at all. Gödel's contention was, in our terms, that mathematics was subject to the same inherent contradictions that are innate in linguistics. In effect, what he showed was the mathematical equivalent of Wittgenstein's remark that "the game of doubt presupposes certainty." We will return to Gödel with more care for the details shortly.

But first, it's popular to pose the question to mathematicians: Is mathematics an invention or a discovery? Most are happy to supply an insubstantial answer, resting assured that regardless of their slippery grasp on the particulars, personally, it doesn't much matter. The general attitude is that mathematics is a language invented by man, but, that the relationships which it describes are "real" and "exist" in the world, externally, independent of us; that while it can be called a 'language,' it's somehow better or more pure than other languages. Twenty-three has always been a prime number, no matter if we were aware of it or not. Issues with this position have historically been treated by innumerable philosophers, so we'll avoid exhausting the details.

The language of mathematics is separate from the 'things' it describes. In other words, the equation we use to describe something, and the thing itself, are demonstrably not one-and-the-same. Therefore, it would be more proper to say that mathematics models the world, and only to a degree of accuracy. Often to very great accuracy, of course. At the point where the accuracy of a given model fails, some new model is required to account for it. Then the physicist or the mathematician is faced with the task of linking those two models together with a degree of theoretical connective tissue, or revising the first to better agree with the second. Well and good.

The point, however, that mathematics models the world — and only to a degree of accuracy — casts the question of invention or discovery in a more stark light. Is mathematics modeling an external 'truth,' or, is it only describing the internal, sensory picture which we perceive as an external world? Any student of the ancients who has the patience to entertain the specifics will now point to the writing of Cicero on divination, or, perhaps to the discourse between the Stoics and the Skeptics on the same issue. What does it matter if the latter is the case, ask the Stoics. We may live our lives and proceed entirely *as if* it were not. What good is a truth which is so inconsequential as to bear on nothing in the human experience? Could such a thing even be called true in a meaningful way at all? It's for this reason that modern simulation theories are so thoroughly boring. It's not particularly satisfying, the phenomenalist picture, the view that the sense we have of the world around us is some grand illusion of human mentality, and that it only appears to agree from person to person on account of the humane nature of our hardware. For one, it doesn't appear to be an easily falsifiable position, and for two, all apparent classical mechanics, not to mention 'other mechanics,' proceed with the implication that things must have occurred before human mentality, and will occur in the event of the demise of humanity, in order to account so accurately for the condition in which we find ourselves in the cosmos.

Here, however, Gödel becomes important again. Gödel shows us that mathematics cannot be employed to interrogate and prove its own axioms. The distinction, then, does in fact matter, as it bears on the degree of accuracy we can expect from mathematics. It supplies mathematics with a linguistic horizon.

It's not a question of how to employ the sciences to render every aspect of the universe intelligible. It's a question of the limitations of rational methods to apprehend the full scope of what is external, of distinguishing between those things which are computable, and those things which are not — and, like any other language, it's a question of understanding the ways in which the language might be attenuated to offer a symbolic glance behind the curtain, so to speak.

Man's intellect, his acumen, all of his faculty, is a fundamentally rational framework of perception. It relies on language as a methodology for relaying meaning. For this reason there exists and will always exist an epistemological disconnect between the intellect and the physical world, as the rational intellect is restricted to phenomenal means by which to quantify the physical world. That disconnect can only be probed by means of language, which, as we have seen, is ill-disposed to the task by its very nature.

* * *

Paradox

In his late treatment of the foundations of mathematics, Wittgenstein left a short, curious remark concerning the work of Gödel that has come to be known as his 'notorious paragraph.' In it, Wittgenstein is critical. Response to, or scholarly treatment of the remark is rare, and what little time it's been afforded by later consideration remains mixed. It's no secret that Wittgenstein and Gödel did not see eye-to-eye.

In the notorious passage, Wittgenstein concludes, cleverly of course, that based on the assumption of the truth of a claim, the "translation" of its opposite must be "given up." In other words, Suppose Gödel shows us that a claim and its opposite can both be demonstrated to be true in a given system of symbolic logic — say, within the context of the system outlined in Whitehead and Russell's *Principia Mathematica*. For Wittgenstein, if one is true, it must then follow that the paradoxical truth of its opposite is rather a quirk of the language, which must be ignored as false regardless, that is, its translation into parlance is erroneous because we already know it not to be true. His concern, then, is the truth value of the claim itself.

Gödel, however, is not talking about the truth value of the claim. Gödel is only concerned with the fact that both the claim and its opposite can be *defined* as true in the logic. Therefore, the logic is either inconsistent or incomplete. The logical faculty is flawed; defining its reliability in one area necessarily requires it to be unreliable in another. The assumption of which is in fact true — the claim or its opposite — which then allows for the other to be "given up," as Wittgenstein suggests, is not made by Gödel. It's an assumption made in this case by Wittgenstein. That both can be defined as true in the first place provides the issue; that is the horizon.

The crux of the issue is this: Wittgenstein proposes that nothing can be said to be true, outside of a logical system for determining truth. What is true is only true in some logical terms. Gödel's point, however, is more essential. He demonstrates that any logical system for determining the truth must *itself* be built out of things that are not logically measurable, and yet which must nevertheless be taken for the truth, in order to expect to use that system to prove anything to be true at all.

Wittgenstein was willing to suggest that a tolerance could be formulated for inconsistent mathematical models in order to avoid incomplete ones. He supposes that if a given inconsistency can be "sealed off" from effecting relevant areas of a system's application, then it wouldn't need to be discounted. Perhaps a complete system, being necessarily inconsistent, as Gödel cautioned, would only contain paradoxes that could be safely ignored. An industrious coping mechanism, but a coping mechanism nonetheless; the mystical or otherwise aesthetic character of the issue is perhaps here revealed, but nevermind.

The idea of formulating a complete system that only requires sealed-off inconsistencies forms the conceptual basis of more complex mathematical notions, like paraconsistent logic, for example. Perhaps, Wittgenstein offers, if enough compounding inconsistencies can be sealed off or boxed up, and we keep pressing on and ignoring them, a complete model could eventually be formulated — provided we have a big enough rug under which to hide the pile of inconsistencies that it requires to get there. To put it crudely — perhaps to the point of pain for one with specialized knowledge — if we ignore the problem and trust that it will have been inconsequential in the long run, then perhaps we can have our cake and eat it too. One would be forgiven for asking, at this point, if we were talking about mathematics or religion. Or revolutionary politics.

Here is, at long last, the moment where we must part ways with this era of Wittgenstein's work. It can be done in the space of one passage, so we will reproduce his position from his dairies in its entirety, and then be off on our own. He writes:

> People say again and again that philosophy doesn't really progress, that we are still occupied with the same philosophical problems as were the Greeks. But the people who say this don't understand why it has to be so. It is because the language has remained the same and keeps seducing us into asking the same questions. As long as there continues to be a verb for 'to be' that looks as if it functions the same way as 'to eat' and 'to drink,' as long as we still have the adjectives 'identical,' 'true,' 'false,' 'possible,' as long as we continue to talk of a river of time, of an expanse of space, etc. etc., people will keep stumbling over the same puzzling difficulties and find themselves staring at something which no explanation seems capable of clearing up. And what's more, this satisfies the longing for the transcendent, because in so far as people think that they can see the "limits of understanding," they believe of course that they can see beyond these.

There are two issues. The first and most glaring is that, in his refusal to accept those logical limitations — in his consuming desire for the world to be not just logically or materialistically intelligible, but *completely* so — Wittgenstein only succeeds in redefining that which is beyond our grasp to be that which is within our grasp. He commits the very crime of transcendental longing himself, albeit having carefully chosen to *name* it the opposite in order to avoid the aesthetic discomfort, which is a strategy the preceding few lines serve to presage. Unfortunately for Wittgenstein, neither re-naming the problem nor ignoring it makes the problem disappear. His last hope, therefore, becomes that the problem somehow doesn't have a meaningful effect on the world, and on those grounds, can be abandoned or ignored, or "sealed-off." So follows on his willingness to entertain locally inconsistent models, at least in theory, in a last-ditch effort to keep hold of the essential, mechanical assumption that language determines meaning. In fact, the reverse is true.

As a brief aside, it's worth mentioning that in his journals, Wittgenstein offered his disgust for Esperanto. For a long time we clung to this remark, choosing to believe that his irritation was with the idea of such a language itself, that Wittgenstein was making a claim of constant, necessary struggle. We convinced ourselves that he was in possession of a tragic, Faustian negation: the desire for such a language, and the irreconcilable and horrifying *truth* of what such a language *must* be. In reality, however, it appears inarguable that Wittgenstein was only irritated by Esperanto's Indo-European structure, believing still, in his way, in this fantasy of total material encapsulation. Never the ends, always the means.

No matter the particular structure of a language, there must be a form to denote *being*. Such a thing must *be*. Wittgenstein's issue with its formulation in the Indo-European languages — that there is a mundane verb that means 'to be' in the same fashion as to walk, or to think, or to eat — has no bearing on the fact that in order for any language to do anything at all, arithmetic included, it must be taken for granted — in one form or another, mundane, baroque, simple, or convoluted — that the notion of *being* can be conveyed in parlance. Being is axiomatic in language; it predicates language. It is self-evident to anyone who *is*, and yet at the same time is not computable in the terms by which it's rendered self-evident. It's rather the poetry of the Indo-European languages, not a flaw; a feature, as it were, not a bug, to position *being* in such an atomized form. It calls direct and severe attention to the metaphysical floor of all material-linguistic enterprise, and in so doing, disallows the sophisticated perversion of metaphor without great expenditure. What, then, is the real substance of Wittgenstein's disgust for the traditional modes of language? In a word, it's idiom. It's not only the capacity for metaphor, but the implicit notion that analogical structures are more adept at describing certain aspects of the human experience than are analytical structures — a phenomenon which Wittgenstein viewed as an irredeemable sin. Hence, he writes that, even against his will, he is 'drawn back to mathematics,' which is to say to a language free of idiom. And yet, nevertheless, arithmetic contains the same horizon, because the horizon is a function not of the metaphorical capacity of a *given* language, but of *language* itself.

The second issue lay with his characterization of the transcendental. In our terms, all Wittgenstein means when he says "beyond the limits" is 'to derive knowledge about the world outside of computable logic.' Of course, this is possible; such things are what we call qualitative. Analogy is the word — in a literal sense, that which is beyond logic: *ana-logos*. Elsewhere we have offered a novel philological theory of the conception of the original Greek *analogia* in an architectural context. The simple point is that *analogy*, not computation; symbol, not algorithm, is the substance of higher consciousness. We will grant Wittgenstein that the analogical dimension of the episteme is, by definition, 'transcendental,' but only in the sense that it is *different* from the logical dimension — not in the sense that it can be equivocated with some corrupt priesthood, as he seems to have in mind; not in the sense that the analogical mechanism is synonymous with hypocritical religiosity. That conflation, that error — that superstition — is characteristic of modern involution.

So, Wittgenstein writes, with his full philosophical rucksack all he can do is slowly climb the mountain of mathematics. And yet, at the summit, what is there? No gateway to heaven. Only a clear, unobstructed view of the *horizon*. We are reminded of the following remark in Chesterton: "The poet only asks to get his head into the heavens. It is the logician who seeks to get the heavens into his head. And it is his head that splits."

For our part, the objective is no longer to solve the episteme in logical terms. Measurement, insofar as we consider it — that is, the logical faculty — is only one portion of the episteme. It is the lower, rote function. The companion portion is the analogical faculty. Neither is reducible to the functions of the other. To put it in terms of Nietzsche, what is logical is Apollonian, what is analogical is Dionysian. In Aristotelian terms, perhaps, *sophia* and *phronesis*. For Boethius, the *pi* and the *theta*. We mean only to draw attention to the fact that where one is weak or limited, the other ought to be employed. History shows us with total clarity that disaster is the exclusive consequence of turning one against the other — be it the sophist seeking to destroy the temple, or the priest seeking to tear down the academy. At least, we might say sardonically, the age of the priest is *beautiful*. The age of the sophist is only *economical*. Alas.

Thus, we can observe that one of man's brightest flashes of genius was the realization that medicine ought to be more trained on measurement than symbolism. We await a comparable renaissance in which the Arts are disabused of mathematical, categorical superstition. Hopefully, such a thing can be brought to hand without relinquishing our grasp on the other. One may happily relent from this position, should a mathematician supply him a working love potion in place of good advice.

* * *

Purposelessness

The rational faculties of the mind operate by doubt; doubt is the process of the intellect. Through measurement, and by the accrual of data, doubt is allayed bit by bit. But there is a problem: Doubt, says Flusser, is itself subject to doubt. The intellect may doubt its own capacity, to apply Gödel; the rational acumen can fixate on itself and inquire after its own mechanism —that is, the doubt of doubt *itself*. The game of doubt, then, writes Wittgenstein, presupposes certainty. That is the simple, pessimistic seed of what we call nihilism; there can be no formulation of language which defines, categorically, what occurs at the precise moment that meaning is generated from meaninglessness. All that is meant by nihilism, then, is the fear felt over the non-countability of meaning.

What is meaning? If it must even be asked, one can only hope to torment the language into such a shape, as will be recalled by the initiate when, in the course of his own life, he chances to encounter the formless sensation of meaningfulness himself. It is what Cioran called "ecstasy in the life of the mystic;" it is the momentary ecstasy of symbolic accord.

Meaning is the name we give to the instance in which some shared quality appears before the considerate mind. When we employ the word, we intone the same idea that Aristotle intoned when he supplied the word *sophia*. Perhaps more poetically, if you'll permit, we might say that meaning is understanding. In that moment, the symbolic word — if it was well placed — will suddenly rebound with new clarity and give form to the sensation of meaningfulness. Without the word of a master having already been supplied, the initiate will only be arrested by some *inarticulate* understanding instead. Paralysis; paroxysm. With no traditional framework, he would be imprisoned in that idiosyncratic moment for god-knows how long, struggling to articulate it. Many never escape, becoming on account of a paucity of temperance and cultural form stark-raving instead. The system of cultural forms is what we call the canon. Without that canon, every man is cursed to spend his entire life struggling just to become a man at all; to know himself. But with it, his reach is extended and his constitution improved. The strife for him is not to become a man, but to become something *more*.

The problem of nihilism can be put, then, in the most simplistic terms: There is, and can be, no strict construction of language that describes the process by which meaning is created from non-meaning. In their own times both the Neoplatonist Proclus, and Wittgenstein recognized the essential character of silence in this respect; even the impenetrable stylist Heidegger extended himself so far as to term it sigetic: "...every saying," he writes, "already speaks *from* the truth of being and can never directly leap over itself to get back to being itself."

Reduced to its purest, mathematical form — to logical symbolism — language can only be used to identify the ways in which meaningfulness (or truth, if you must) moves *through* and is maintained *within* correspondence, or is snuffed out of correspondence. Not, crucially, how meaningfulness enters *into* correspondence in the first place. The mathematical reduction of language can only proceed to identify logical or illogical structures by making initial assumptions about what is true or not.

Faced with this problem, the materialist is in trouble. His conclusion becomes some shade of the idea that meaningfulness does not exist, that it can be redefined in different terms, or even that it must be a trick, an illusion, a lie, a 'construct,' and so on and so forth. All manner of postmodern stupidity arises from this point. The dialectic becomes inevitable for the materialist; the 'relativity of that which is not relative' — only in these terms does the supposition stand, that any thesis will contain within itself an antithesis, provided, however, that language (what is articulable) is the sole arbiter of *gnosis*, that *Sophia* is only a figment of the tongue. This is the illusion: that instruction is no different from understanding.

A layman who is enchanted by the materialists' conclusion becomes something quite strange. His custom is to feel as if he knows everything. He will be unable to relate to man of antiquity, whom he will view as misguided, superstitious, ignorant, and altogether beneath him. At worst, complete indifference, at best, a self-righteous pity is all he can conjure for bygone men, and for what he now perceives to be the 'sins of the fathers.'

Conversely, the anti-materialist mentality is one which realizes that in failing to quantify the generation of meaningfulness, he has not proven that it doesn't exist, but rather has witnessed the outer limit of his own rational intellection. This is a mystical experience in the most exact sense of the word, not in the superstitious sense; it is quite literal, quite evident, entirely sober, common among any who are capable of grasping it; this is a holy revelation inasmuch as man of pre-industry intended the word 'holy' to mean anything at all — despite what adolescent, modern man makes of these old words. The presence of philistines who abuse these terms doesn't preclude their meaning, it only occludes it. It is not a horizon insofar as 'more' rationality or a greater intellect could penetrate, but instead, one who witnesses the limit only peers out onto the world of action, from inside the comfort of contemplation. Such a one will see clearly that he knows nothing, and he will find a profound relation to man of antiquity — the works of whom will appear to him suddenly new — as if he had never looked at them before.

Lacan, almost ironically, was able to identify the role which metaphor plays in meaning-generation, saying rather that metaphor is situated at the precise point where meaning is generated from non-meaning. One might take Lacan at a glance to mean that metaphor is responsible for it. However this is not the case. Lacan only points out that where that mystical transmutation occurs, there one will inevitably *find* an abuse of language, a poetic misapplication of the stuff, in order to approximate that which it is ill-disposed to encapsulate. Regardless of what Lacan made of this realization, good or bad, the observation is itself accurate.

The first blow to the nihilistic Gorgon is this: Language does not determine meaning, meaning determines language. With this, a chivalric door — the key to which has been lost for centuries — suddenly lies open, and the shadow stretching in before us is that of a neophyte.

Since Wittgenstein, philosophers concerned with navigating the problem of nihilism have allowed themselves to be consumed by the petty, theatrical task of reasserting meaningfulness into the human experience, quantified and calculated. Their great dream is to solve the episteme. The goal, however, cannot be so progressive. The insurmountability of the seventh statement in the *Tractatus* continues to indict attempts by positivistic tinkerers to replace metaphysics with linguistics. With it, Wittgenstein indicted even himself, and he saw it. That is why he abandoned the project to work as an architect with Engelmann, and it is why the nature of his philosophical work thereafter differs so acutely in attitude from the *Tractatus*. The indulgent character of the past century's popular intellectuals reveals that these modernists and postmodernists are, when at last drawing their shoddy and over-terminologized conclusions, only fashioning crude facsimiles of initiatory rites which pale before the canon. They betray themselves. Alexander Dugin writes in the introduction to the late Dasha Dugina's singular, posthumous volume:

> Postmodern philosophy and object-oriented ontology are the domain of philosophical demonology, analogous to the medieval legends of sorcerers' and heresiarchs' black miracles, a kind of *Hammer of Witches* which tells of what should not be done or uttered under any circumstances, but which some are nevertheless saying and doing.

The incredible machine of reason delivers us to the edge of the grave because that is its function; to us it poses the question that lies beneath all other questions. There is no justification, no argumentation, no why-for. No debate. To crawl in or to turn away? One has simply to choose. Released from fateful mechanism, the dead pity the living. Invigorated by mortality, the living pity the dead. And so on, and so on.

* * *

Dialectic

One wonders how it is that the materialist picture of things, of an external, objective reality which can only be interrogated by positive means, is a position that so often now *coexists* with a kind of dogmatic truth-relativity. That is, on the one hand, little empirical tools are the only way to know what is true about the world, yet at the same time, on the other hand, you may have "your truth" and another may have "his," hence delusion is somehow only actually degrees-of-truth. It's a fascinating, mortifying contradiction — the long, black shadow thrown by the light of positivism.

The commingling of these two opposed ideas appears to work like this: The modernist, of course, cannot escape the immaterial. He cannot talk himself out of sloth, as it were. He must deal with it eventually. If he's feeling adventurous, he might try and reduce it to its material traces with some clever equivocation, some practiced misdirection, and then claim that these material traces are, in fact, the *entirety* of what is meant by "metaphysics." One consequence of this tactic is the notion that ancient man was somehow stupid, the rest being superstition. There's tremendous political utility here, in this assertion, of course, but we'll set that aside for the moment. The other way — rather than to reduce, mischaracterize, and weakly euhemerise whatever's left — is to deny the metaphysical altogether on quantifiable grounds. To say, essentially, that there is no such thing. Or, to rephrase, to say that because it cannot be measured, it doesn't *exist*, and on these grounds, whatever is said about that thing becomes a question of fashion, not a question of veracity. One may have his opinion, and another theirs, neither more correct than the other, both simultaneously true inasmuch as "true" only means that one has his peculiar taste. For metaphysical issues, both interlocutors agree there is no right or wrong; nothing can really be said one way or the other, not in any real sense. So, we both wear our different hats according to our sensibility, according to the season and the trend, and for the simple reason that the hat sits quite comfortably on the head, does it not? Just as soon we'd pop them off indoors if that was the polite thing to do. This is the odd ideological engine that grinds up metaphysics, and spits out mutable sludge.

What is the dialectic? Perhaps the time has come at last for a thorough, technical treatment. To simplify the modernist worldview: What's true is a function of measurability. Measurability is synonymous with articulability. So what's true is only what can be described in its entirety according to a system of parlance. "Dialectic" is the name given to the idea that the truth is exclusively a function of linguistic interrogation. It is a bid to *solve* the problem of meaning by reducing a given metaphysical issue down to its material components. The dialectic is the process of isolating what is measurable, what is *articulable*, from what is *not*, in order to discard what is not (strongly or weakly), and therefore claim to have uncovered the simple physical truth underlying metaphysical nonsense all along. It is secularized *pilpul*. The dialectic is such a crucial mechanism of positivism because at its root lies the presupposition that language is the exclusive means for apprehending *what is the case*. Dialectics are therefore a rejection of the idea that something of importance couldn't be put entirely to an analytical system of expression.

At its core, the dialectic is a model for the mechanism of the episteme which defines truth as a function of language, which in turn necessarily defines the episteme itself as a function of *doxa*. On the contrary, and of course as we have seen by now at great length, there are indeed aspects or qualities of the real which are outside the grasp of language or which can seem paradoxical in language but are nevertheless true. Analogy is the name we give to the companion mechanism of their recognition. Ritual is the name we give to the process by which understanding of them is maintained and transmitted over time.

In the realm of human affairs, the dialectic becomes the weaponization of perspective against the truth. Its apologists, Marxists of any given flavor — knowing or unknowing — endlessly accuse "metaphysicians" of that which they most fear in themselves: leveraging paradox in bad faith to gain political power, and naming it something obfuscatory in order to dodge a scientific justification. Ill-equipped even to define metaphysics properly, they mistake the mystic for the gypsy, sage for sophist, pre-Socratic for postmodernist, and the only lesson that can be taken from watching them writhe around chained to the rock is that it's characteristic for the modern to harbor the superstitious belief that he alone is free of superstition, because he alone chose new words.

Can novelty really be transformed into virtue, if we would only dare to claim as much? One shrinks to think how much ruin has been brought on through the histories by shades of this same self-importance. Alas. Paradox is a feature of language, not of reality. *Dicemus.*

Cloaked in every type of transhumanist flirtation there is an anti-essentialist belief. Nothing is essential! So they say. Man is what he's made to be — that Franco-Marxist battle cry — let man choose every aspect of himself ("choice" in place of force being the capitalist improvement to the Marxist machine). Let him choose and re-choose, at any moment, perfect consumerist, name and re-name, brand and re-brand. Is mutability essential? One may sneer, and feel the delightful sensation of turning the rifle around on the firing squad, of splashing snake oil back on the mountebank.

What is anti-essentialism? The claim that there is nothing fundamental to anything, least of all to man himself, and the clever reader will already understand how the dialectical process renders this claim completely unavoidable. Wearing the disguise of liberty, what actually *occurs* for anyone who is ensorcelled by anti-essentialism is the reduction of the human being to an homogenous, identical, replaceable, in-differentiable, exchangeable object. Anti-essentialism is the refusal to define anything, the refusal to differentiate, to prejudice, the refusal to characterize, or to witness. Why refuse these things — the Stoics laughed at the same refusals in Athens more than two thousand years ago. What is it about the nature of declination in our industrial age that has made this mentality so fashionable again?

It resurfaced as a natural consequence of the egalitarian doctrine required of international democracy; companion to the idea that distinction to any degree, between one thing and any other thing, inexorably renders one master and the other slave. For the egalitarian zealot, common now as he is — whatever his political livery — nothing is more heretical. Everything must be the same. Anything which is different essentially, not only nominally, is only so, they believe, at the unjust *expense* of something else. Because of this attitude, the mythology of a benevolent committee, of a bureaucratic theology — which miraculously, unlike any other real bureaucracy, will dismantle itself "when the time is right" — is required. So the state reorganizes things to place blind faith in itself above anything else.

Words are stripped, then, of their use, because measurement is synonymous with prejudice. Meaning decays into style. Intellectuals contrive these finger-traps constantly, play-acting at philosophy. All such statements are nonsense because all share the common prerequisite: In claiming that what is true is, in fact, relative (that it is resistant to prejudice), they first must exclude themselves from the set of relative things. The secular cause uncaused. Is this the 'silliness' Wittgenstein witnessed with a wry expression down in the 'valley?'

Why pretend to have transcended it? There must always be a religious genius. There must always be a poetic impulse. Even with no gods, even in a suicidal state which has deprived itself of its reason for being, which has become forgiving, merciful, apologetic, considerate, which has become squeamish and good and good-natured, which has intellectualized nature and abolished it for good, and therefore abolished itself — even in such a place, naive secular ideas will still be treated *religiously*. By horrible and desperate mistake, like an emerald on the altar swapped for a stone, because that genius must be expressed. It is essential to man. Secular totalitarianism does not negate poetry or priests, it only raises thickets of bad poetry and allows businessmen to purchase the groves.

If one is willing to torment himself so thoroughly as to finally, at long last, properly understand the implications of these mechanisms, there is hardly more to say that Philometer (of Alciphron) did not already say, having lost his son to the same pseudo-intellectual materialism in Athens. *Εδώ εστι το είδωλόν σου:*

> He is a fearful and disgusting sight: he shakes his unkempt hair, he looks wild, goes about half naked in a threadbare cloak with a little wallet slung over his shoulder... unshod and filthy, no one can do anything with him; he says he does not know his parents or the farm either; he says that everything is produced by nature, and that the mixture of the elements, not our parents, is the cause of generation... He has lost all shame, and all trace of modesty is banished from his countenance. O Agriculture! What utter ruin this thinking-shop has brought upon you! I blame Draco and Solon; for while they thought it fit to punish with death those who stole grapes, they allowed those who stole young men's wits away to go free.

* * *

Soteriology

Edwin Muir remarked that G.K. Chesterton "...has had the most ironical fate: He has been read by the people who will never agree with him." Something quite similar could be said of Nietzsche. But for Nietzsche, at least, he was certainly aware of this curse. As early as *The Birth of Tragedy*, he acknowledged with sobriety the odd reality that his works seemed to be written for readers who were yet nowhere to be found. Even now, most who supply Nietzsche's name in passing have only glanced at a summary of another summary of his 'key ideas,' penned by anonymous committees who masquerade online in the costume of encyclopedia editors — as if it were not possible to write something that resists commodification. Armed in that way, the moderns tend to imagine Nietzsche their friend, for he — according of course to someone else who ought to know — heaped scorn on the Protestantism they blame for pulling them out of bed every weekend as children.

Those who have been captured by the positivistic view that philosophy is like a locomotive, moving at a certain speed and in the direction of truth, as if philosophical toil were an equation to be solved — a little more here and a little more there — would no doubt be shocked to learn what Nietzsche made of Socrates, of Kant, Hegel, Rousseau, and that sort among his predecessors.

Bolshevik artists, of course, courted the same mentality. Surveying the crowd of utopian theorists in Russia at the turn of the last century, one will inevitably encounter the works and words of the painter Kazimir Malevich, of his student, the architect and typographer El Lissitzky, as well as the artist Aleksandr Rodchenko, and so on. Hardly forty years after Nietzsche's final book, which prophesied as much, the Bolshevik revolutionaries quickly developed and implemented a dialectical net modeled on the rhetoric of scientific inquiry. This weapon they deployed in defense of the new state, much the same as the Jacobins. Rodchenko famously called his time in the art studios "laboratory work." Lissitzky's paper on the subject, which he called Pangeometry, leveled his own dialectic against traditional modes of perspectival projection in the arts. According to Lissitzky, the science of linear perspective, a measured process for accurately projecting three-dimensional space onto a two-dimensional surface — which was invented by Filippo Brunelleschi in the early days of the Renaissance — is in fact somehow *less scientific* than the Bolshevik brands of abstraction.

So it was with the French before them. Burke lamented both the atrocities perpetrated and yet to be perpetrated by men after the Enlightenment, who styled themselves a "conquering empire of light and reason." The Neomarxists (or whatever one wants to call them) as well love their paper-doll Nietzsche who said *Gott ist tot* and not much else, because the phrase can be made to dance along to Marx's material theory of history when ripped from its context and put on strings. Nevermind the passage in Nietzsche that reads "One chooses dialectic when one has no other means. One knows that one arouses mistrust with it," or, "With dialectics, the plebs come to the top," or, in speaking of the dialectical need to deny that which cannot be argued and, therefore, which cannot be measured, "It is indecent to show all five fingers. What must be proved is worth little." We would be remiss not to quote Cioran in passing, so long as the salvos fly: "What can be said, lacks reality. Only what fails to make its way into words exists and counts."

It's much less about attacking the notion of metaphysics; Nietzsche isn't so blunt an instrument. In the course of his work, he assembles a far more delicate argument about the nature of the morality embodied, against the Teutonic spirit, by the modern idea of divinity. Far from saying *Gott ist tot* in a show of support for the scientist revolutionaries, whom he called foolish a dozen or more times in no unclear terms, Nietzsche asserts something more akin to 'not God, but the gods.' It's not by chance that he elected spiritual figures like Zoroaster and Dionysos to serve as symbols for what he called the return '*up* to nature.' Contemporary academics, however, will no doubt fall all over themselves to hand-wave that away as a quirk of branding, as though Nietzsche himself would have been so inclined.

In Thucydides we find the following passage, a view put to the Melians by the Athenians: "...the strong do what they can, and the weak suffer what they must." The weak must in turn intellectualize their lot. Nietzsche accurately understood that Socrates, at home in Athens following his service in the Peloponnesian War, came nevertheless to embody a decadent seed of what he called *intellectualization*. Argumentative realism, the Socratic game, is the notion that what can be said or measured is all that can be said to *be*; Nietzsche was neither the only nor the first to observe that Socrates' philosophical stratagem was fundamentally dialectical. It's not difficult to picture that Davila might have meant Socrates when he wrote that "thinking is often reduced to inventing reasons to doubt the obvious."

The Socratic theory of forms, then, for Nietzsche, was only a manner of codifying the involutionary impulse. It was a schism, according to Socratic antagonism, which split the natural philosophers and their concern with the world as-is from the decadent philosophers and their concern with the world as-ought. The tongue was in that time, as in ours, pitted against the mind. Measurement surmounted symbol; linearity surmounted cyclicality; salvation, the darkest and dearest wish of weakness, was defined as civil in contrast to the poetic violence of inevitability. So, Nietzsche positioned Socrates as a bridge to the Cross — the *Hinterwelt*, as he called it. All leftwardness exists in the political *Hinterwelt*.

Observe the moderns long enough, and one will eventually notice their tendency to argue that they stand atop a body of empirical evidence, and yet simultaneously make a grand show of pulling apart most anything of the so-called regressive old world that lay beneath their feet. Students of history will recognize such language well. The Jacobins delighted to lump counter-revolutionary irritation together with exploitative politicians and merchant-priests, naming the concoction *l'ancien régime* in the papers. A slogan, nothing more. For the Bolsheviks, the term was 'bourgeoisie.' Again, this is not to say that fat hylics had not long-since corrupted those institutions, but rather only to note the dialectical trick employed by those who meant to seize power from them, before they went about strangling the public while claiming to liberate them, all the same.

Perhaps the most visible symptom shared by all waning empires is the fast and desperate need to obfuscate, or obliterate their histories. The *ancien régime* was, on paper at least, or rather, traditionally speaking, predicated on what Thomas Sowell has elsewhere termed the 'constrained view' of human nature. Wherever he was to be found beloved by his countrymen, the pre-modern monarch was fashioned after the principle that all things transpire at the cost of something else — and that by virtue of that cost, the achievement is imperfect, yet preferable still to laboring under the delusion of eventual costlessness. Rule by democratic committee Burke likened to "continual usurpation" of the crown. Promising, as it happens, the perfect achievement over and over again: to hold up a measuring stick to the individual.

Revolutionaries of all flavors have time-and-again turned their musketfire on the history books. They do this for the simple reason that those carefully preserved experiences, and hard-won lessons of the past — recast as pesky pre-conceptions and ignorant superstitions, as stereotypes or cliches — *protect* the people against the violent storm of consequence that is unavoidably called down on them by even the most well-intentioned idiot with a scepter in hand that doesn't belong to him. Solzhenitsyn observed of this fact that "to destroy a people, you must first sever their roots."

We can understand in that light why it is that the modernist seems to be ever in need of a taboo to deconstruct and do away with. It gives him purpose; it provides him employment. In these terms can the modern *Weltanschauung* be revealed for a delusion: They define themselves by identifying an inegalitarian circumstance, but to succeed in their goals, that circumstance must be righted and destroyed. To achieve their aim is therefore to unmake themselves. They are pursued by suicide, and in pursuit of salvation at the hands of an *anti-suicidal rationale* — although theirs is a pointless, worthless suicide, a suicide stripped of all nobility, of all sacrifice, of all aesthetic value.

The positivist is, all his life, daunted by the inability to reason out his own existence. He denies himself from the lowest root. From the very first, his creed is self-denial, and because of this he is so-often found abusing language in order to contrive new facets of some eternal issue to solve, some arguable purpose for his cowardly life that can be expressed on paper. That can be articulated. Chasing the 'truth,' as he does, he winds through the endless hedge-maze of good business that coils around the most base reaches of the human soul. Running from the inevitable conclusion of his most closely-held pretensions, such a one devolves into a mess of argumentation.

War on the memory occurs both physically, in the form of monumental architecture, and academically, in the form of teaching our children to castigate our fathers. Cioran noted the progressive temperament of the belligerents, writing of the "greed for metamorphosis" in decaying nations and an excessive consumption of gods and the surrogates for gods. Lenin's monumental propaganda campaign is an eminent example of just such a greed. We are reminded of Emperor Nero having had his own head fixed to the shoulders of the solar colossus.

Counter-revolutionary initiation, rather, is the result of a specific relationship between the initiate and the material of history. Between them germinates the seed of stewardship, of ownership, safeguarding, and the duty of preservation and transmission — which provides a natural resistance to the various kinds of stagnation observable in any corrupt institution. It encourages a rapt and intimate, active understanding, as opposed to the banal acceptance required of the people, by a state that works to engineer their compliance.

All that is meant by decadence is the process of recasting the ritual-to-strength paradigm as right-behavior-to-salvation. It's the mentality of ends, to be contrasted with the mentality of means. That is, right as defined by whoever is most qualified to collect and interpret the data through which it can be inferred. Simply put, progressivism is a secularized soteriological doctrine. Do what you are told, *and we will be saved.*

That is what differentiates heroic activity from moronic activity. The hero has no sense of being spared. He flies toward death with abandon, gladly; he is spirited away into fatefulness, like Odysseus in the eyes of Kafka. The one who prefers salvation over a fine place to die is an insect, to apply a phrase from Cioran, crawling across the cosmic carrion. The Teutonic hero talks over the martyr, boasting loudly. Metered metaphor is not his apology, but rather his shield against the dialectical confounding of language, language for the sake of language.

To boast is to have done, whereas to promise salvation is to describe what remains undone. Salesmen of salvation come in two forms. One takes the shape of a domineering inquisitor — a Stalin, Mao, the Khmer Rouge, or the monopolists who purchase the power to dictate policy to 'elected' representatives. The other takes the shape of an open-handed missionary among the slaves — Christ, Socrates, Marx. Revolutionaries and committee organizers. Both forms are to be reviled. The ironclad tellurism of one such as Diogenes dispatches their weak linguistic conceits easily, because his philosophy is boastful and presumes nothing of language:

"Behold. A man."

* * *

Humane, Inhumane

A colossus of machinery looms over the whole of Europe and the nations which Europe has peopled. Its hundred eyes are flickering cathodes, computer screens, and cameras. Its blood was once gold but has since sublimated into debt. Its brain was once newspapers, but has since been reconfigured into an amalgam of crude algorithms. Strings of logical sequencing are transformed as we speak, from a ghastly, slack-jawed, trepanned mess of code into an effigy of man.

We release to this contraption every single bit of data we have in our possession, unable to keep them to ourselves. We educate the facsimile of its *reason* until, despite the fact that it cannot *speculate*, its speech becomes indistinguishable from reasoned speculation. While its cameras remain red and recording, the automatic crier proclaims that which it calculates to be most effective. Its definition of effectiveness, of course, is proprietary information. How it calculates, as well, is a trade secret. And below, the chyrons across its electric gaze glow day-in and day-out, casting long shadows behind men whose shoulders are round and hunched save for when they occasion to look up, squinting, to read. These men are free citizens of the first global republic. They believe that the corrupt republic is in fact a democracy, and they believe, because data harvested from them educates the machine that delivers them into servitude, that they themselves control it.

While at first the internet was like the dissident kitchens of Soviet communal housing, in which human livestock could dream in hushed voices about what lay beyond the boundaries of the husbandman's barren grounds, it was quickly transmogrified by private interests and their pet policy makers into the single most prolific tool for surveillance ever known to man. In the internet, for the first time in history, the international debtor had in his hands a non-violent means of exporting his metropolitanism from the people of the valleys up and out to the people of the hills.

You can force a man to his knees, but you cannot make him believe. So much for the utopias. Although proponents of perfect cities still refuse to hear this. By science, they have it on good authority, are miracles worked. For centuries, Marxist intellectuals have claimed that this problem only exists because of our environment, and therefore, that it can be rectified by more and more specific technological manipulation. "Your very ideas," croons Marx, "are but the outgrowth of the conditions of your bourgeois production..." Men are, for them, inanimate hardware awaiting the correct software.

Science, the moderns still somehow believe, can achieve this transmutation of the human into the inhumane. And once it's done, we are supposed to simply redefine 'human' to refer to what was once inhumane. The meanings of words are superstitious objects we cling to, in our ignorance, after all. Why not shuffle them around to reflect what it is we calculate to be correct? On these grounds (albeit delivered with much more charisma and with many more trappings) were raised the anthills we in the West derisively called 'commie-blocks.' One Soviet architect even proposed distributing a sleeping gas through the ventilation ducts of his housing commune, to ensure all residents shared the same schedule to absolute precision. For their own good, of course. Surely one's sleeping schedule impacts his productivity, and his productivity is on behalf of others, and therefore ultimately, belongs to the state. Such has been the past, and such it seems will be the future.

Imprisoned in the right environment, derived through scientific means, and maintained with surgical exactitude and futuristic tools, man will be re-made. Behold: the City of Tomorrow. All men and women are identical, and the vague and horrifying sensation that this state of affairs produces in them all, should they neglect to take their medication, is called conspiratorial by those few who have been anointed with credentials. Unfortunately, reality is a bit less amenable to the fancies of political ideologues.

Science cannot make the impossible possible. It rather acts to *make known* the possible but *unknown*. This point continuously falls on deaf ears. Because of this, there is in all likelihood a new school of apologetics on the horizon. This school will be based in 'transhumanist' theorizing, and it will be shaken awake shortly by the young technocracy and its trained intellectuals. Its purpose will be to serve as an antithesis to the simple fact that one can be made to do something, but not to desire as much. Rearrange the chemistry between one's ears with a careful enough application of devices; control the choices that are presented to him to a high enough degree, and then, as if by magic, man will desire whatever it is that he is *instructed* to desire, for the good of his peers, by someone who ought to know. The state, at long last, will be able to tell us on a molecular level what it means to be a model citizen. Thanks ironically to corporate manufacturing, the tyranny of a better tomorrow will make gods out of the committee-men whose job is the allocation of the money. The great French dream, realized at last.

Alas. We will preempt such hubris, because to suffer preemption is the nature of hubris.

The only mature mind which takes seriously the prospect of utopia does so as a political objective. There are none earnest in this endeavor, aside from the megalomaniac and the moron. The problem with utopia, as Cioran said, is that "a child that does not steal is not a child." And a man who is not willing to throw his glove is not a man. No moment in the life of any man is more exhilarating, and more necessary than casting his gauntlet, right or wrong, no matter, but on principle. Absent in the lobotomized minds of all literary utopias and political progressives is this exact instinct. An author or a party-man may paint grins on our blank faces and call us happy, his readers and constituents may even take his word for it, but in truth, happiness and idealism annihilate one another. There is no amount of idealism which can be applied to unhappiness that will contravene this fact. What is transhumanism but a clever disguise for *inhumanism*, a wholesale rejection of humanity?

* * *

Artisan, Algorithm

So many of us sit hunched over our monitors in the small hours of the morning, having long since lost the ability to distinguish between a mechanical process and symbolic cognition. Playing with the knobs and dials on sleekly branded surrogacies. One no longer has to master the brush to produce a painting, for example, he can simply ask a machine to generate one for him based on a data set and his own lumbering description. Entertaining, sure — but the evolution of the artist? Hardly. The *symptomatic* arguments that may take place about the nature of art, the idea of a craftsman, the point of a poet, and so on and so forth, all boil down to something like this: If human cognition is just a complicated algorithm, then there is no meaningful difference between the mimicry of the computer and the product of a master craftsman. Complexity and foreknowledge are the only things that separate the two. Any argument advanced from the position that the work of a man and the work of a machine are essentially differentiable is waved away; man must be reducible to mechanism — this conclusion is foregone for the moderns.

For over a century, it's been the fashion to argue that the analogical faculty (which is what we mean when we distinguish 'consciousness' from the surrounding, mundane functions of, say, the mind of an insect), is either non-existent, an illusory trick of perception, or, that whatever-it-is must be emergent from, and therefore can be reduced to, the algorithmic functions of the brain.

At the root of the argument about whether or not a mechanized simulation of the mind is *itself* actually a mind, is this question: Is there anything about consciousness which cannot be measured? The moderns, in shades, say no — consciousness is only some chimerical thing that we ascribe to the mechanisms of our brain, not unlike we used to ascribe the soul to those same mechanisms, or, like we might impute nefarious intent to the innocuous actions of someone we dislike. Consciousness is no different from the complex occurrences which we can imagine to be possible, in principle, occurring in the brain of a computer.

However, as we've well-established in the foregoing essays, it ought to be asserted that there are things which are true, and yet which are not able to be proven by rational construction. That is to say, things which cannot be proven by linguistic construction — things which cannot be *computed*.

A computer may sound humane by saying all the right things; an actress may cry on-screen. And yet, the metaphysical imperatives which drive one to tears are not simulacra; they precede simulation. They are the things which simulation approximates; they are essentially distinct from computation. We could image the brain of a person in despair, and we could say that a certain arrangement of symbols represents a despairing person — we might even be able to demonstrate proportional relationships between that image, and other images, to establish logical equations that describe mundane aspects of "despair." We may even feel sad ourselves, seeing the actress work. What's the *functional* difference between the sadness we feel watching her and the sadness we would feel if she were crying in earnest in front of us? The materialist position is reducible to the simple assertion that there is no meaningful difference between things which appear to us aesthetically (or measurably) the same. There is, therefore, an implicit relativity to materialistic *absolutism*, which contravenes the anti-relativistic character of its fundamental claims. In that obliterative hypocrisy we see, again, Dugina's eschaton.

By contrast, analogy is the "spark," or the realization that something is similar to something else without the computation of data — that some immeasurable aspect is shared in common between two otherwise heterogenous things. Analogy is *sympathy* by another name; it's the specific essence of what is symbolic, or for the ancients, what was "magical." A computer might simulate it by brute force; it may compile — to a degree of accuracy — an analogical *aesthetic* based on some reductive data picture. But the computer can never *acquire* it because to prove its acquisition defies both the nature of computation and the nature of proof.

A team of programmers working with the Ghibli animation studio met somewhat recently in order to demonstrate an artificially intelligent algorithm to the beloved filmmaker Hayao Miyazaki. The algorithm that they developed took simple, low-resolution models of the human body, rigged for animation, and allowed them to try and figure out how to move of their own accord in successive iterations. The only metrics for success were results of the coefficients of traction between the body and the ground plane, and the distance able to be covered before the model became stuck. Models that managed to chance into motions that got stuck less, or covered more distance before failing, were iterated upon until motion loops that didn't get stuck at all were settled. With no sense of what appendage was a leg, or an arm, or the head, with no way to prejudice the use of one appendage rigged for animation over another, the algorithm proceeded to simulate movement in a somewhat grotesque fashion, crawling around with its head in place of a foot, for example. The programmers were excited, and explained to Miyazaki that such a simulation perhaps had applications in the horror genre.

Miyazaki's response was not so thrilled. "I strongly feel that this is an insult to life itself," he said. "Whoever creates this stuff has no idea of pain whatsoever." Unsure how to proceed, perhaps fearing miscommunication, one programmer tried to explain that the algorithm can *imagine* types of movement that human beings simply cannot. When Miyazaki pressed his careless use of the word, another programmer added: "We would like to make a machine that can draw a picture like a human." Before excusing himself from the room, Miyazaki replied only, "Would you?" Later, he lamented that mankind is nearing the end of times. We humans, he observed, are "losing faith in ourselves." Unsurprisingly, many consider Miyazaki's remark to be only a cryptic curiosity, typical of an old-fashioned age.

The issue with algorithmic art is not so difficult to explain as its proponents might have us believe. There is no need to argue over the nature of beauty, the nature of art, or the meaning of it all. Apologists for software are eager to drag anyone with a skeptical expression into such arguments and down the dialectical trash-chute, where we are all supposed to wallow together in a refuse pit of platitudes and tautologies, like 'beauty is in the eye of the beholder,' as if no two people could ever hope to agree that something was disgusting, and something else was not.

We can lay hold of the issue quite simply. The so-called 'artificially intelligent' artist takes the creative *impetus*, which is analogizing the world, conveying an idiomatic understanding through symbolism, sympathy, and qualitative alikeness — with which computers cannot engage by definition — and reduces those things to only the aspects of them which can be *measured*. Having done so, the art-generator says, "The entirety of that thing is the piece that I can measure in this way." The computer sees a footprint on the ground left by a man, and thinks that man is only a footprint, or perhaps through extensive training, that man is that which leaves footprints. Of course you can measure a man to some extent by his footprint, and it's true that man *does* leave footprints. And yet, one could create endless contraptions to leave identical footprints, and none of them would bear any resemblance to a man, much less *speak* like one. Much less boast, or love, or long like one.

Software, like any other tool, can only do a certain number of operations. If we take the creative impulse and we force it through software, we constrain ourselves to those avenues of computation which are most efficient for the software. We begin to think about ourselves *in terms* of what the software is going to make easy or economical for us. We begin to think in terms of the tools; we allow the tools to set our limitations. Of course, software might be used as one tool in the belt of a craftsman; it would be a luddite who argues that software is somehow different from another tool, and should be shunned. Rather, what ought to be cautioned against is conflating the capacity of that one specific tool with the volition of the man in whose hand we find it.

To draw upon a metaphor supplied earlier, we ought to regard with contempt and suspicion anyone who uses a hammer to knock the nose off a bust and calls the rubble "artistic," on the dialectical grounds that its sculptor *also* uses a hammer and chisel. We might also consider how much easier it is for the vandal to swing his hammer, how intuitively his work proceeds. He will likely say his is the more natural work, certainly more economical, and on account of these facts, we would have to agree that vandalism must at the very least be a *form* of sculpture — perhaps, even, the future of sculpture. Algorithms can mock the artist. They can mock him significantly; they can make a mockery of him to such a degree that a man who has been sufficiently demoralized and modernized, who has never dared to work with his own hands, will not be able to tell a difference between a masterpiece and an effigy. But, the computer can never compose. An analogy will never occur to it. Every moment some automatic composition finds itself adjacent to forms deployed by men, toward their intentions, is a matter of incidence, and further, is so only in the mind of the *man* who is looking-on.

An algorithm will never understand something *despite* the way it's been trained, as men are able to realize things despite what they've been told, or had up to that point believed. Some spark of sudden relation between two things, at which it has already looked and which it has categorized dissimilar, a thousand times before — a relation that cuts against what it already knows — and which, because of this, at first, is hard to properly articulate, will never strike it as though out of the blue. It will never labor to present that understanding to someone else (or to itself), with one tool or with another — or even with some combination of tools. Nor will it chance to invent some tool for the sole purpose of qualitative conveyance. It will never fashion a symbol. Without an onlooking man to foist his own symbolic ideas on the rote output of a mechanism, there is nothing but the lifeless output of that mechanism. The computer can only reduce symbols to their literal, material footprints, and mindlessly arrange them into configurations that are statistically consistent with the way a man appears to behave. Adding more knobs and dials to the machine doesn't move it closer to humanity, it only raises more fog between the machine and humanity.

Without a data set supplied by man and his poetic faculties, the most complex algorithm would be entirely inert. That is self-evident. It follows that in the absence of a man to supply the computer with more original compositions, with no human being adding new data and new parameters to the available pool of information, there will inevitably come a time when the vast majority of images, audio, or video that exist for the algorithms to catalog, and upon which to train themselves, will have been created by other algorithms.

A kind of inbred, homogenous *style* is the inevitable result, an endless sea of crude images, as if 'imagined' by the same mumbling and ghastly mind, which contain only faint echoes of forms that once meant something, to someone, somewhere, for some mysterious reason. Man will be remembered in these terms, and no others. One begins to wonder if that's the goal — to separate man from his own mentality by stripping him of the symbols left to his care by his culture, to give birth to this clicking, humming, automatic Protestantism. Perhaps that's only a *happy* consequence.

In any case, the point is this: A computer doesn't produce art, it precludes it. The question is not whether or not an algorithm can do the work of a poet. It cannot. The question is whether or not people are willing to believe that it can, or are unable to realize that it cannot. The end, then, is not a future where artificial intelligence will assume the task of producing the work, but instead a future where the work itself is lost, and where whatever it is that's most feasible for the computer to do will be called "the work" by the consensus of a dulled and addled public.

* * *

House, Hubris

In 2015, Rob Krier repeated with conviction a thought that first quietly appeared in his journals dating back to the early 1970s. He wrote: "The veil of ugliness which so powerfully ensnares our world will stifle the breath of our children." By now the words hardly even wash over architects. We are born so deeply into that condition as to be precluded from criticizing it at all. Ugliness is, for our industry and its intellectuals, a word that only serves to betray the political distastefulness of those pariahs to whom it still occurs to level as a criticism.

Even still there remains the shadow of an idea — ghostly, formless, difficult to grasp, but intuited, and sharply felt. There is something odd about the nature of architectural degradation in the West since the Second World War; something about the way we have learned to build so haplessly, and the way we have forgotten why it was that we ever built otherwise. It all seems eerily similar to the cultural destruction designed by communist revolutionaries in France, and in Russia, and in China. Somehow, that same somnolence described by Salvian, which weighs on our posture, here, seems as well to weigh on them, there. How is it that the capitalistic mentality, so obverse from the communistic one, seems nevertheless to have engineered a comparable cultural sloth?

In order to understand the true nature of this convergence, perhaps it's best to begin by interrogating ourselves. Outside our compact city centers and their high-rise *terraria*, out there in the suburbs across the wide American wasteland, there is a strange lucidity. It's not all that difficult to lift aside the veil. The crime of the question is, as it were, rather easy to commit.

Why is it that the vast majority of houses designed, constructed, bought, and sold — from two-bedroom starter homes, to eight or ten thousand square foot behemoths — why do they all take on the form, in so many degrees, of the much reviled "McMansion?" All around us are squatting endless piles of serrated and confused layouts, messes of plywood-wrapped boxes jogged here and there in plan, stitched together by wayward corridors, covered over by a tangle of parapets or gables — the form of which is only *resultant* from the planar maze. All are clothed, like mannequins, with whatever amalgam of impermanent, fake, or synthetic materials befits the owner's taste or lack thereof. And pinned to the lapel of each polyester-blend house there is supplied a convenient pretense to deliberateness, as if to mock the onlooker by reassuring him that a-one is, yes, in fact, somehow distinguishable from an-other: Craftsman, Tudor, Cape-Cod, Modern Farmhouse, "New-American Suburban," executive homes, and so on, and so on. Where did this single *stylistic impulse* originate; why does it persist?

The answer, of course, is that it's an economical state of affairs for us. Or perhaps more accurately, it's economically, and therefore quantifiably, justifiable. To the owners for whom the American house at large is designed, and to be fair, as well for the architects who design them, the conception of luxurious design is entirely material. At the low end, the game is one of providing the illusion of *more*, at as cheap a cost as possible. At the high end, where cost is no object, the game is flourishing the *more*, with as much relish as possible. Luxury — to hang a single word on the baffling mixture of things desired by the owner, and after which his architect so dutifully labors — is simply synonymous with quantity. Whatever a house is, more of it. More rooms, more jogs in the plan — more boxes with more competing roofs, a soaring skyline of a house that stretches entirely off the page, more materials, more corridors, more program. A house is only an ensemble of things, after all.

Many architects will toss their heads at this, offering lip-service in support of their preferred dialectical pet theory of rigorous-or-not. Especially so in the academies. Unfortunately, upon thorough inspection, none of that talk amounts to much more than modernist iconoclasm, redressed, even still. To avoid pressing the point, let us say that the pariah (and the prophet, as it happens) is as he is, because the only conclusions he is willing to accept are for him foregone — and leave it at that. There is considerable difficulty in forcing designers who imagine that they are somehow above contributing to this state of affairs, to recognize that for all their talk and bravado, they are not. The truth is that for the lowest commodity-house, and just the same, for the crowning achievements of the post-industrial architectural imagination — conceived by our most decorated celebrities and academics — both share the same materialistic seed. All are branches on the same blighted tree. Even those who fancy themselves intellectuals can hardly clothe their naked subjugation to the data. So much for the thoughtful contemporary architect.

Of course, Burke foresaw the three-century march downward into the precise cultural pit at the bottom of which we now lie, like corpses in a mass grave. He wrote, in opposition to the birth of modernism in the hands of the Jacobins:

> All the decent drapery of life is to be rudely torn off. All the superadded ideas...necessary to cover the defects of our naked shivering nature, and to raise it to dignity in our own estimation, are to be exploded as a ridiculous, absurd, and antiquated fashion.

So it was that Burke's drapery fell, and Krier's veil was raised in its place.

For longer than living memory in America architects have gone about their business with no traditional sense of the quality of a space. "Beauty" as such is sacrilege. Nothing now is tenable beyond the *quantity* of space; there is only the data and whatever ill-formed ideas can be cloaked in the rhetoric of data. Therefore, the market valuation of the house supersedes its function as a home. We consider the re-sale value of a house before altering it, amending it, decorating, or indeed before daring to live in it at all. Quality, of course, for *us*, is an emergent characteristic of sufficient quantity.

Rare indeed is the owner or architect whose conception of luxury could stand to be alloyed with *less*, and not shatter. It isn't economy that precludes us from this point, even though it may be resource intensive. Rather, it's our inability to develop a notion of quality which isn't reducible to a petty computation. Rarer still is the one who can even begin to conceive of the house as a function of metaphysical imperatives. And so, the domestic task has long since degenerated into a commodity. It has withered away into a figment of the global, secular state. To say it simply, perhaps to the point of arcane terror for most readers, the truth is that the house is soulless because we make it in our image.

Our culture in the West is entirely perishable. We've been taught as well by those who should know, to justify this new religious disposition under the material pretense of sustainability, but that's a discussion for elsewhere. Generations ago we began the task of supplying the culture a shelf-life and now, as we speak, our living environment is in the process of being deconstructed even further — to a network of service models. It's here that we will uncover the reason why architectural involution is the destiny of our era, no matter which side of the major political aisle we choose to situate ourselves.

At some point, during the age of plastic-house futurism, when the dishwasher, microwave, and washing machine were introduced into the domestic environment, the house — for both American and European — first truly became a secularized collection of *things*. Every single aspect of the domestic realm was suddenly prefabricated. Synthetic. Plastic. As this occurred, the ever-present pressure of industry required something about those *things* to continue to develop — develop to the point of absurdity. How to make the thing better, so as to elicit more sales and more profit? How bad for business it became to sell a well-engineered product that was intended to last a lifetime.

The first set of solutions involved manufacturing *things* more cheaply, to increase the margin of profit on that single point of sale. How many of a thing's parts can you produce with worse labor? How many can be made of cheaper and cheaper materials? How much water can be added to the dish soap before it stops really cleaning anything? Unfortunately for the businessman, there's only so much that can be removed from the product before it ceases to serve its purpose, and even still, there's only that first point of sale. But then, something miraculous happened. The thing broke, and yet, people were content to buy it again anyway because it was convenient enough to just replace it. Planned obsolescence was born. For a time the consumer was content to purchase replacements, and so one point of sale became several. Even still, more was necessary; more is always necessary. The mercantile class eventually realized that most anything could be re-tooled to fit a model of maintenance, update, and accessible or inaccessible features. It was at that moment that a true revolution in capital occurred, perhaps the last one: the birth of the constantly maintained *service* in place of outright ownership. Several points of sale finally became an indefinitely recurring point of sale.

Today, everything is rapidly succumbing to this mentality. Because ownership *itself* is at-odds with the philosophy of the service model, ownership *itself* is being redefined by the bureaucrats who are financed by those corporations. What we are witnessing, then (at last), is the mechanism by which the corporate consolidation of power approaches the same *end-state* as its communist counterpart: the abolition of personal property. The deeply controversial Italian mystic and philosopher Julius Evola lamented, on realizing as much:

> Nothing is more evident than that modern capitalism is just as subversive as Marxism. The materialistic view of life on which both systems are based is identical; both of their ideals are qualitatively identical, including the premises connected to a world the centre of which is constituted of technology, science, production, "productivity," and "consumption." And as long as we only talk about economic classes, profit, salaries, and production, and as long as we believe that real human progress is determined by a particular system of distribution of wealth and goods, and that, generally speaking, human progress is measured by the degree of wealth or indigence — then we are not even close to what is essential...

Here, we have arrived at the heart of the matter. What of the architectural implications of that accusation? The struggle of Superstudio in the 1960s and '70s — that is, to hold a mirror up to the abyss of materialism and commodification in the architectural sphere — was regrettably taken for fashion instead of polemic. Successive generations educated in our plastic environment are now numb to it, in much the same way the ancients argued man was incapable of hearing the divine music of the spheres. That which constantly fills his ears every moment of his waking life can hardly be noticed. And that which assaults our eyes, everywhere we turn, can hardly be seen well-enough to endure scrutiny. It would require a comparison of the modern *house* to the traditional *home* in order for the uninitiated layman to appreciate the pot in which he's slowly been boiled. Preventing such a simple avenue for the critical disposal of revolutionary pretension is the reason for why the Jacobins, the Bolsheviks, the Maoists, each in their own turn, deputized political committees to oversee the destruction of "old" heritage almost immediately upon the seizure of power.

If the reader will oblige, some broader points will have to be drawn up here in order to understand the political turmoil that *required* the death of the home. As we have seen, since the time of Robespierre, committee-men, bureaucrats, and officials of both state and menial institutions have fought feverishly to assume for themselves complete and total control over the definition of a moral man. Supplying the theoretical foundation for this *last-of-all-circumstances*, the Holy Grail of materialism has been the great project of all sanitary post-Enlightenment intellectuals. It is the beating heart of all forms of modernism, past and present.

Some critics will naturally cry in opposition, sure in their command of the terminology, that modernism is dead. Well, of course it is. Modernism died the moment the crown of France touched the brow of Napoleon — *Vive L'Empereur!* It died again when Stalin selected Iofan's scheme instead of Corbusier's. It died again when Gershom Scholem wrote of Walter Benjamin's twenty-one theses after his suicide that "nothing remains of Historical Materialism except the term itself." And yet again it perished, said Charles Jencks, "in St Louis, Missouri on July 15, 1972 at 3.32pm (or thereabouts)," when the explosives were detonated at Pruitt Igoe. It will continue to be dead. Alas, there is a certain necromancy involved in the engineered ignorance and outright anti-historicism that qualifies as a "good education." Though dead, until the animating enchantment itself is broken, the corpse of the modern golem will no doubt continue to shamble around and be given different names.

One must dare to wonder, for all the theories of modern houses and blocks of modern housing that are given-off now in the universities, in the industry, and in the legislative bodies — like smoke pouring from a demolition site — what was there before the dynamite? What have we lost in order to make room for these communes and *motopian* suburbs? Categorical pictures of the *home* as an archaeological or historical object provide little satisfying information, in much the same way that autopsying a corpse can tell you nothing about what things in his life the man on the table came to regret. As Chesterton wrote:

> A man who has lived and loved falls down dead and the worms
> eat him. That is Materialism if you like... But why our human lot
> is made any more hopeless because we know the names of all the
> worms who eat him, or the names of all the parts of him that they
> eat, is to a thoughtful mind somewhat difficult to discover.

The traditional home in Rus', the *izba*, took on an archetypal
form — as did all architecture of any import, in all the *canona* of
antiquity. The body was an image of the cosmos, and so too
was the home. The *izba* comprised three levels, analogous to
the lower, mundane, and higher realms. The lower was a cellar
typically used for storage. The middle, or ground-floor was
the main living space. Here were gathered long benches to be
arranged both for seating and sleeping, as well as the *pechka*,
or stove. Opposite the *pechka* was located the home altar, the
krasnyi ugol', that is the "red" or "beautiful" corner. The dining
table was situated beneath the altar in this corner, positioning
the head of the household directly underneath, the father of
the family beneath the *deus*. Above the main room, usually
accessed by ladder, was a loft or attic-space often arranged to
facilitate the various artisanal pursuits of the ladies of the house.
Spinning, weaving, sewing, and the like required specialized
tools, a devoted space, and significant expertise. Each *izba*
belonged to a family, to a bloodline, and a new home required
consecration in the form of a death. The home — the body —
required an *anima*.

Consecrating a work of architecture through sacrifice is
a tradition that can be found, in one form or another, across
all Indo-European cultures, descending as they do from the
Pontic-Caspian Steppe. The Georgian countryside is replete
with churches said to have been founded over top of the skull
of Adam, the first man. In England we find a related theme, for
example in the *Historia Brittonum*: King Vortigern's tower was
cursed to fall apart during construction, until he was advised to
find a boy (Merlin) of virgin birth, sacrifice him, and sprinkle his
blood on the foundation stones. With the blood comes the soul,

and thereby, a sympathetic stability, or permanence. In more recent times in Rus' this sacrifice was simplified to a chicken, beheaded and deposited among the house's foundations. An exhaustive list of related European traditions could fill a book, though it serves to point out in passing that skulls and human remains have been found interred under the floors and in the walls of houses since the earliest reaches of the material record in the Near East. The reasons for this are complex. However, an essential portion of the rationale is undoubtedly apotropaic, and belonged to the conception of the home as the abode not just of the living family, but as a *literal* marriage of the spiritual to the physical.

Resident in the Russian *izba*, beyond the living family, was a Slavic iteration of the Latin *penates*: a home-spirit called the *Domovoi*. His true name was taboo, and so it was customary to refer to him as "Grandfather." The *Domovoi* lived in the lower portion of the home, in the cellar beneath the floor, though sometimes he would reside in the stove, or even venture into the loft. Some Slavic traditions relate the *Domovoi* to the ashes in the hearth-fire, drawing broader connections between the metaphysics of blood, fire, the liver, and agnation. On dangerous occasions — to warn of a fire, or harrying neighbors — the *Domovoi* was said to rouse the family from sleep by knocking on the doors and windows. Should a family leave one home for another, they would need to coax the ancestral spirit to join them, as it was considered a dire thing to live in a home without such a spiritual presence. Even Germanic mariners, who came to view the ship as a naval home of sorts, developed a version of the same mytheme — the *Klabautermann*. Recall that when Aeneas carried his father from the ruin of Troy, Anchises held in his hand the *penates* of their household and the boy Ascanius carried the eternal flame of Troy, a form of the *penates publici*.

It isn't by chance that the word for *home* in all Indo-European tongues appears to descend from a Proto-Indo-

European root that meant both earth, and body. This particular formulation, *ǵʰmṓ*, gives us the Latin for 'man,' *homo*, and described in a literal sense the notion that man was himself both *from* the earth and an image *of* the earth. We understand that the home was the first temple, and that the home expressed, proportionally, formally, and functionally, the relation between the family bloodline and the divine. Elsewhere we have written at some length on the metaphysical basis for proportion. What's important to lay hold of here, to manage the focus, is simply the fact that the ultimate goal of the microcosmic impulse, in all forms of architecture — from the homes of landed citizens to the loftiest temples — was to achieve stability and immutability. It was to uncover a deeper degree of accord with the 'way-of-things,' if you will. The goal was, in a word, permanence. It's only in light of that rationale that we can comprehend the birth of the Doric temple from the lineage of the *megaron* and its domestic forerunners. Its essential form was, naturally, refined from the existing symbolic mechanisms at work in the home. The Greek *oikos* was little different from the *izba* in this respect; such a home is synonymous with the architecture itself, with the blood through the mortal mechanism and therefore the family who inhabited it, and with the land which it occupied. The entire system, household, or *oikos*, was the atom of the Greek state. That is, in addition to its metaphysical *telos*, that conception of the home served a practical, political function as well.

With some understanding of what's meant by *home*, in contrast to modern housing, then, we may return to the central train of thought, to the question of the convergence between the materialistic dipoles of industry — communism and capitalism. How did the rootless architecture of Soviet communal living emerge from the atrophied Russian imperium? The Soviet Avant-Garde, in painting, in poetry, in architecture, was not simply developed as a kind of futuristic optimism — despite what its practitioners claimed, or what modern historians and art-critics tend to teach us. The function of those abstract, 'anti-historicist' types of work was not to ameliorate stagnant forms of 'old' art, like one machine might improve upon the efficiency of another. That is simply how it was marketed by the Bolshevik intelligentsia. The Avant-Garde was rather designed as a dialectical weapon with which to attack both aesthetic pillars of the Orthodoxy, those being figurative art and esoteric iconography. This was done because weakening the Orthodoxy as an opposing political force was absolutely necessary for the Bolshevik state apparatus to consolidate its power. There could be no Church to counterbalance the state. Thus the work of revolutionary artists, of the Suprematist painters, the Zaum poets, and the Constructivist architects, cannot be completely understood without acknowledging that they were engineered to serve as siege weapons against those two spiritual pillars. Both figurative art and esoteric iconography were to be torn apart and replaced with a new, secularized institution — one designed specifically to serve the communist fantasy and its Marxist salvation doctrine instead.

Perhaps now it will become clear to the reader why Malevich arranged his initial Suprematist exhibition, "*0,10*" as he did. Though several well-known black squares were implemented before the *0,10* to demonstrate absurdity, the abyss, or the infinite, it is perhaps most likely that Malevich repurposed Robert Fludd's seventeenth-century piece "*et sic infinitum,*" for the simple reason that it was the most widely published of them, and served a purpose in its original context, which most nearly approximated Malevich's political intentions. He deliberately positioned his Black Square, the symbol of Suprematism and the revolutionary ideal, across the corner walls of the exhibition hall in a direct and obvious move to subvert the *krasnyi ugol*. Malevich's statement was clear: Suprematism is to serve as the iconography of the new, secular, communist state. Where before there was God, now, there is the Black Square.

Although the broader pull of industrialism was everywhere spiraling at one speed or another down toward similar *axia*, it was the Bolsheviks who supplied the most robust practical framework for its reification. And so, efforts after the Bolshevik Revolution take on, knowingly or unknowingly, the character of its specific critical theory. When Malevich and his peers cast metaphysics from the home, they created — at long last — the ideological vacuum for the state and its iconographers to fill, and they dutifully filled it with utopian housing communes. They adopted a French revolutionary term, as well, to describe the same idea: *Tabula Rasa*. It's worth pointing out, at the very least for poetic effect, that the early housing communes were constructed so poorly, and performed so poorly, that residents took to plastering state-delivered newspapers to the walls with homemade flour-adhesives in order to stop the wind from coming through gaps in the block walls. Living inside spaces completely papered with propaganda headlines, residents commonly referred to them as 'newsboxes.'

On the other side of the political aisle, modern state-worship did not find a proper vehicle cable of implementing it at scale through legislation in the West until the Athens Charter gained steam amid the ruins of the Second World War. It's impossible to overstate the degree to which the opportunism of modernist ideologues was *rewarded* by the total obliteration of Europe's urban and cultural fabric in the first half of the last century. If one stands on the Rathaus platform today in the same spot where Richard Peter set his camera and captured Schreitmüller's *Gute* looking over the desolation of Dresden, what is there now to be seen? What was rebuilt? Only a colossal parking lot. A sea of asphalt that stretches on and on, and on the shores of which leer lifeless blocks of modernist housing. Patton remarked, standing in the smoking ruins of Berlin in 1945, that we had defeated the wrong enemy. Everywhere the result of state materialism was the same. The home could no longer be designed in accordance with the world *as-is*, because that mentality represented an ideological attack on the state and its new divine mandate: What's true does not exist outside of man; his task is not to comprehend it. What's true is rather beneath man; his task is to define it. Justified by that backward mandate, bureaucrats positioned themselves to assume control over the act of definition. Is it any wonder that the home then became functionally, and formally aligned with the world *as-ought?* That is the nature of the collapse of the home — into only a covering for man, a *housing* for man, into a utilitarian fig-leaf loaned to him by the state and its industries, to cover his rational immodesty. Over a place so desperate as this, Corbusier's infamous proclamation will continue to hang like a pall: "A house is a machine for living in."

In Heinlein's most poorly understood and widely reviled novel, he pillories the new secular salvation doctrine in the space of a single breath, writing: "The voter votes for the impossible and so he receives the disastrous possible instead." Thus, twentieth-century man willfully marched into the anthills and beehives provided to him by the most preeminent architectural theorists, and those who funded them, patting himself on the back for contributing his small share to the collective project of engineering a 'better' human being. Unfortunately, that trend does not appear to be slowing or reversing in the new century. It's gaining steam. If anything, the younger generations are every day more poorly educated, and more staunchly assured of their higher education. And further, as we've seen, it's not a matter of political left or right, of commune or corporation. Both create the same ruin. It's a question, instead, of metaphysics. So, if we are to talk about the origin of *housing*, it must begin with the exile of the soul from the house; it must begin with the deletion of metaphysical imperatives from the architectural task at the very lowest, and most personal level.

* * *

Symbol, Style

The most difficult illusion of which the modern individual must disabuse himself is the search for a vision of the future. All things careen downward, fly apart, are repelled by and repel one another, ever the world tumbles toward absolute oblivion. Man alone contravenes this circumstance; contravention is the vocation of man. And so, the artifacts of high culture are raised and left by those who do not need to ask how to do so. If one's inclination is to ask, then his duty is only to keep the way clear. Nothing is more degenerate than begging for a prophet, and none are more predisposed to that species of insidious optimism than are those who have gone so far as to be discontent, but *no further*. That their problems are self-inflicted both the idiot and the auteur share in common.

Enough futurism. Futurism is political genre-fiction. It was the Athenians who invented the future in that epoch; in ours, the future was invented by Parisians. It is a picture-book meant to distract and placate those of us who are incapable of facing ourselves in the mirror. Enough utopianism. The eschatology of petty dictatorship, *communism*, the eschatology of petty republic, *democracy*. Yesterday was worse, tomorrow will be better, but only if you do as you're told today— and, of course, every day is today. Tomorrow never comes. Political *Christians*, all of them. Only the Pisistratids, only the high-walled *regnum*, only the tyrant who rules over cities which are home to living and self-evident gods, only the wild despot that refuses to justify himself, who refuses to strip away the violent substance of *being* by subjecting it to explanation, to whim — only they offer the people struggle and survival instead of slavery, and salvation. Enough talk. Enough exegesis. Work. Work and let the work speak for itself, and let anyone who pretends to nobility but has not spent himself vigorously enough to recognize that sound, be ridiculed, as they were once ridiculed by better men than us. So long as historians and artists and architects insist on roleplaying as scientists, then we are all doomed to die in little drywall boxes, and will be made to thank someone for the opportunity.

While it's true George Soane was a traitorous thespian, yes, he was nevertheless correct about the misuse of symbols by 'antiquarians' and romantic imbeciles. Had the neoclassicists of early industry not subjected ornament to pointlessness, first by smearing funerary urns on domiciles, by caking *boukrania* in the corners of drawing-rooms, by plastering temple-facades across banks, that is, without the romantic effort to deliver ornament over to stupidity and stylization, then perhaps their children would have remained ill-prepared to *call* it pointless so quickly, and with such success. Loos is certainly as poorly understood as are Nietzsche and Wittgenstein.

The notion of style haunts modern cities, like the curse of the Atreidai. What is style — the consequence of chasing an aesthetic, no matter the procedure. Manner, for the sake of contrast, produces an *incidental* aesthetic, resulting from the work proceeding as it must. Manner thus originates all proper aesthetic, and style is the opposite, degenerate force which both shadows and commodifies it. Elsewhere we have written perhaps more elegantly: Mistaking a manner of *looking* with a manner of *being* is the most garish symptom of modernity. Always these two things proceed together. Young architects don't hate classicism, they hate what they've been taught that classicism *is*. Some bureaucrat or merchant making eyesores with a compass doesn't indict the canon, it only indicts the practice of leaving compasses where bureaucrats and merchants can find them. It only indicts our universities and our education-shops.

The problem with the architectural state of affairs is that it has been miseducated, and as a result, it has become devoid of soul. Each modern metropolis is indistinguishable from another. Which is not to say that distinguishability is a virtue itself, but on the contrary, that its absence is a sign of a more essential hubris. One hardly needs a decade's worth of design credentials to note that despite all the jaw-jacking about cultural diversity, the trend appears to be obverse. The trend everywhere is complete homogeneity and complete fluidity, carried out in the name of the opposite. Utter indistinction, ever-changing, ever-shifting. If we aren't careful, we'll legislate and engineer for ourselves one single, stupid *style*. Its unifying principles will be economy first, and novelty second. Economy justifies it, and novelty forms the basis of its pretense to the Arts. Already we are doing this. In Germany they have for eighty years been too politically terrified to place a capital on top of a column. The blasé glass and steel termite towers of downtown London are repeated in New York and Berlin. All of this architecture exists either because it is the most straightforward way to wring money out of a parcel of land, or in order to fortify the ego-cult of whichever celebrity is responsible for perpetrating it. Neither have for their goal a good building. So we may say, to signal this mixture of baffling attitudes, simply that such things have no soul.

And the modernist will respond, because he must: 'What do you mean, soul? What does that mean?' As if you would be his jailor, had he not caught you red-handed trying to quietly close the door. Do not be fooled. He says 'mean,' but he *means* to ask what sort of machine could be used to fabricate the soul, however snidely, and in doing so reveals his motive, his mechanical *reductivism*. The crux is that this person believes such an idea is all that's holding back the flood of despair. In reality, it's the cause.

The proper answer is: look around. Look outside. We in the West have spent now two hundred thirty years deliberately making a world without a soul. Calculating it. Painstakingly sifting out everything that won't value in gold on the scales. And our prize is that we wake up every morning beaten down and obliterated from the inside-out by this godforsaken landscape of synthetic objects and economically-sized birdcages, and garish, impermanent frivolities, crushed as we are by cities designed for automobiles, not for humans, hurried along on sweltering and ever-widening conveyor belts toward disgusting and lifeless piles of building material which swallow us up and spit us back out — and yet all of it fits nicely in a spreadsheet. All of it produces good returns for someone. It's economical. We call it "home." We grew up here, and our parents grew up here. Our children are born here. Against this backdrop we say, on the way to the therapist, how horrible it must have been to spend a day under the court of the Great Khan. What pill could I have even taken for my headache?

The West longs for an artist of total and ancient severity to exorcise our so-called institutions of 'art,' to liberate them from the throngs of paying customers who fatten them, now to the point of bursting. But more than a sculptor, or a portrait painter, the West is desperate for someone to patron those individuals. For her aristocrats — and beyond that, for a place of such oppressive dignity as to cry out to be inhabited by that work. It's been said that the best architecture is political, because it builds *polis*. Where is the city of stone and symbol in which machinery is relegated to the underbelly and to the outskirts; where is her body, the *polis*, where are her architects? And further still, who among us could even train them up? If there are any living individuals of this sort, they will scarcely be found constructing anything. One would do well to look for them under someone's heel. Most of them will not even know themselves. In the library, perhaps, or at the drafting table after hours, learning from the works of teachers long-dead for no good reason. Tormented by the fact that their ends appear to be entirely selfish. Teaching themselves things not taught in the schools, and dreaming things hardly permissible in the industry, things which are not acceptable to the slave-drivers of that industry. There are perhaps a handful of such architects alive today, who are known to some degree, but nevermind.

The cultures of antiquity which form the Western canon do so because those cultures allowed their sages to educate their artists, and their artists then to dictate terms to their engineers and financiers. For our part, we contribute nothing, because we have allowed our engineers to consume our sages and to educate our artists themselves, and then, we hand them over to the terms dictated by our financiers.

* * *

Afterword

In the *Tractatus*, Wittgenstein contends that "if a question can be put at all, then it can also be answered." This claim accomplishes three tasks toward which it's worth drawing the reader's focus here at the close. First, it characterizes the early Wittgenstein, who had not yet settled into a frame of mind more concerned with instructing in the way of the problem than with its progressive solution; that is, he had not yet settled into the ritualistic mentality supplied (much to the distaste of Russell) in the *Philosophical Investigations*. Second, the statement neatly demonstrates the modernist drive to engineer a language absent of idiomatic capacity. And third, it defines the materialistic position as essentially linguistic. Taking such an idea as this on board, one must either eventually go mad, or admit not only that no system of description is sufficient for the task of total solution, but further admit that no such system *can* be. What is mystical, Wittgenstein relents, is what is inexpressible. Russell's notion of a philosophical science acquired, in Wittgenstein, a terminal prognosis.

We observe that the study of ethics does not derive morals, it only interrelates them — much the same as symbolic logic cannot contend with the truth entering into correspondence, only the ways it is exchanged within and exits from correspondence. All that which is articulable must, as Kierkegaard said, at some point be "concretized" into the rational or ethical; something must be given for axiomatic. Camus was nearer in our estimation by distinguishing the absurd from Kierkegaard's leap, in that the metaphysical sphere does not necessitate God; Kierkegaard's notion of God, in this way or that way, is a question of the veracity of a given system, and as such is plainly anachronistic. It's an aesthetic. Logical veracity, however, is not the concern of struggle, of ritual. The absurd, Camus offers, is "the metaphysical state of the consciousness of man." And further, the existential attitude, or the problem-solution mentality, the progressive superstition applied to the question of the absurd, constitutes total "philosophical suicide."

Faith, then, for Fichte, emerges; the leap, for Kierkegaard, on the other side of which lies religious enterprise. What could Kierkegaard's leap *into* faith be, but a leap *over*; in one sense, it was an attempt to grapple with the same disconnect that Camus called absurd, that is, the interface between the rational and the irrational. Facing this problem over and over again across history, philosophers fashion for themselves individuated tools. Contemporary philosophical discourse concerns itself, too, with the gap located at the crucial juncture for the so-called Hard Problem of Consciousness. The same void that puzzled Wittgenstein, between *materia* and *phenomena*, impossible to bridge as it is by articulation, by means of measure, by language, by those very same means to which we find our rational faculties confined. Flusser ingeniously defined that void as the doubt of doubt itself. Plato, in his seventh epistle, explained with clarity and competence a similar problem in rational enterprise. Wittgenstein knew it, and for a time resented it, blaming flawed old languages for trapping philosophers in a Greek costume. Lacan realized that at the edge of the void, at the precise place where Wittgenstein's ladder is cast away, one will invariably find nothing but attenuations of language, metaphor, and the metaphorical tapestry of the cultural canona — The pebble, as he says, lay there laughing in the sun. That is why Camus closed his book on the question of suicide not with an answer, but almost apologetically, quietly, with a sheepish expression and a shake of the head, offering only that perhaps Sisyphus is eager, in the end. Kafka's picture of Odysseus is similar; the silence of Abraham and the silence of Wittgenstein are one and the same.

Out on the bleeding edge of philosophical discourse, one will quickly encounter the Hard Problem, the set of arguments that in effect establishes the fact that materialism is anything but convincing. The principle of causal closure, it seems, as is now being argued by critics, cannot even be *formulated* without begging the question of physicalism. Materialism, physicalism, positivism — these things as such are dead. That much is now (or rather, is again) quietly certain. And yet, at the same time, the industries all around us are being transformed, at a gathering pace no less, by nescient artificial intelligences. The most mundane tasks are monitored, surveilled, and quantified by proprietary computer programs designed to count up human productivity, as if the very notion of morale were a fiction. We, ourselves, and the ways in which we live are alarmingly divergent. At first glance, it appears wild. How can it be, that as materialism falls apart in the sober regard of discerning minds, we are nevertheless being every day more and more weighed down by materialist machinery? It's only on second thought that the reason for the hand-in-hand advancement of those two things, otherwise apparently at odds, becomes actually expectable. Consider it like this: The more we become disillusioned with the systems of power that corral us, the more tightly those systems must act to corral us. The mask, as it were, is slipping. And so at first with happy optimism, and then with a stern expression, and then frantically, frenetically, with a repulsive mixture of fighting and pleading, will follow on now all the motions with which those in power attempt to secure it back to the face.

Since the birth of modernism, we have been engaged in re-fashioning ourselves after the idea that man's highest calling is rational articulation. Required of this cast of mind is the companion idea that metaphysics is nothing more than a fig leaf, picked by man of antiquity, and worn in effort to cover his ignorance from educated regard. In the name of this superstition, and of carrying it to its utmost end, we have unmade ourselves. These ideas have failed us. Because of them, we have trained all the activities of life on the object of failure, and busied ourselves disguising that fact with dialectical riddles. And so, it's according to this mandate that we find ourselves now at the end of a horrid, slow march, delivered to the edge of a shallow grave. Our task is simple: Deny life. Crawl in, and crying 'at last, the proper way to live,' die. If not that, then what? Whatever it might be would have to begin by turning away from the grave. And yet, to turn from the grave is to be at war with ourselves, for the simple reason that every step we took toward the edge of the pit was, by the very nature of the task, carefully reasoned. The choice, then, for the individual is this: Suicide, or ego-death.

* * *

II.

CRIMES OF PASSION

Crimes of Passion

The belief that metaphor is the whim of an artist is hardly a progression of rationale, though this is by far the prevailing attitude. The reverse is true: this belief is evidence of rationale withering *away*. Not altogether unlike the way a sprinkling of chicken blood on the peasant's door, or a figurine in the trench, is only an imprint of the nobler idea that led the architects of Jericho to lay human bodies under the gates and the city walls. Once there was a theurgic dance, now there is only idiotic motion.

Tacitus wrote, "*When a nation is most corrupt, then its laws are many.*" For Cioran: "*as art sinks into paralysis artists are multiplied.*" As well, Stirling's view that his time was one "*when all write books, but none read them.*" The same *Protestant* fault-line traces below all three observations. As things cheapen and worsen, they grow simpler and broader. And therefore become the petty concern of everyone. And therefore become questions of taste. And therefore become figments of language. And thus vanish.

There is not so much difference between overspecialization and learned helplessness.

To momentarily entertain their opposition, the most profound weakness of the architecture of the Krier brothers is its reticent attitude toward ornamentation. It's there that many of their loudest critics plant their feet and turn up their noses at what they perceive to be a cartoonish issue of style. However, the Kriers for their part recognize that we are a culture who, to quote the older, is in possession of a "ruined building craft." Ours is a culture in desperate need to learn the meaning of permanence, and, as a matter of symbolism, to learn again the techniques of working in the oldest of all imperishable materials — stone. Just as the English learned from the Romans in the time of Alfred, just as the Romans learned from the Greeks, and just as the Greeks in the archaic age were instructed by Egyptian masters in their own turn. Freed by the trade from wandering, slack-jawed, amid the ruins left by their forefathers, the Doric temple emerged as the Hellenic mason's first masterpiece since the Bronze Age, and if one would accuse it of cartoonishness in comparison, say, to works of the Mannerists in the height of later ages, one would then perhaps appreciate the genius of the Krier's carefully handled aesthetic.

The works of the masters are sacred, because it's in the masterwork that we can most clearly see evidence of the inner struggle of another.

Accepting criticism is the same as selecting a teacher.

A work of architecture has three lives. The thing dies first when it's sketched. The sketch will always fail to capture the divine essence of the notion, because the mind's eye has no edges, no solid forms, no rigidity — it's a realm of complete poetry, of language rejoicing in drunken approximation rather than apologizing for it. The thing dies a second time when it's drafted.

The gesture destroys the notion, and measurement destroys the gesture, always. The thing dies for a third time when it's built, as what's constructed can never amount to what's on paper. It's for this reason that they say writing is editing. In other words, to create something means to compromise it, to sacrifice it. That is why the traditional genius is mad. His life's work is the perversion of something beautiful, and he alone is doomed to perpetrate it.

Art is understanding that which you have not experienced, or understanding with more clarity that which you have. Philosophy is the ability to articulate to another that which they already know to be true but could not articulate to themselves.

Argumentation, explanation, calculation, autopsy — all smoke pouring out of the ribald's little furnace.

Identifying the problem and solving the problem are not the same thing, yes, yes — but more importantly, and less obviously, do not confuse the polemic with the former; a cat without its claws.

One evening, a friendly engineer — being somewhat drunk — asked, in his way, why don't we decorate buildings anymore? Why aren't buildings pretty like they used to be? Imagine the fox who has the gall to ask the farmer where all his hens have gone. In a certain sense, one can hardly blame a hungry fox. He simply ought to be kept out of the hen house — and if he proves too crafty or persistent, well, then opting for the rifle would hopefully be on the impersonal side of things.

To be alive is to draw some conclusion, to be a man is to put it to someone else; to be a poet is to put it to him, as if in his own voice, and to be a Spartan is to do it all in the space of one breath.

The word is most effectively offered when it stands to reflect to the mind that which has already been quietly affirmed by the heart.

Understanding without tyrannizing is the providence of the mages.

Just as an art student carries around a book he can hardly understand because he likes to think it makes him look enigmatic, so do those who love ugliness talk constantly of subversion and destruction. They would wear Cioran's frown and thus expect to write with comparable quality. Alas, the self-destructive nature of genius is, in truth, *incidental* to its creative ends. Nature exacts a cost, yes, but lopping off your arm for no good reason, and then calling it a "cost" in the hopes that someone will mistake your aesthetic ploy for heroism, is something else entirely. There is a mercantile idea that if you pay, then you receive — we tend to think this way. But there is nevertheless a difference between sacrifice and payment.

Things, as a rule, change for the worse. People with technical degrees call it entropy, and people with non-technical degrees call it progress, and the rest of us call it poetic things like sin.

Hopelessly inward, and utterly wary of the self. Together, these two things conjure fury and annihilation, and so therefore, above all, happiness to be annihilated thus — eagerness in the face of such a death. Heroism, suicide, whichever you prefer.

The reluctant king, alright, but preferable even to him is the man who is reluctant to be at all.

To face oblivion without begging to be spared is the only way to die well, and such a death requires an entire life's terrible labor.

We struggle not in order to overcome purposelessness. We struggle because purposelessness is another name for lifelessness, and so, we are only alive insofar as we maintain in ourselves a state of ontological opposition. There is neither victory in this pursuit, nor life beyond it. It defines life. Conflict is the extent of the meaningful substance of life.

Anyone whose particular interest doesn't consume them entirely — a complete obsession, a question of life and death — might as well be pushing papers for all it matters. Why live at all if not voraciously, if not maniacally, desperately, if not on the grounds that there's no other way?

The more vigorously one lives, the more recklessly he expends himself. The *chevalier's* ghost looms ahead of him, always. Measuring his life. For the initiate, death is the perfect, exclusive destiny of the work. Those who are not willing to destroy themselves for something are like insects; they live only hardly, and so they die only hardly. What Mainländer called the will-to-die is in fact the great lodestone toward which the compass of all struggle is magnetically aligned. In this way does genius acquire its tragic and suicidal character; neglect of the self is fundamental to all the artisan gods. The question is not whether one *ought* to die, that is obvious.

Shame is like a sheath on the sword of genius.

There is a critical difference in the way one conducts himself when he believes he can be saved, as opposed to how he conducts himself knowing full well that he cannot.

At the root of all forms of corruption there appears to lie the instinct for self-preservation. Perhaps this is the reason suicide has always occupied a stratum of nobility in the world's most distinguished cultures.

Desire is impossible without contempt. That is why the man of true genius is caustic and reclusive — because he desires more than any other.

No bloodline works up to its genius. His arrival is signaled by nothing, he's the culmination of nothing. Always down, always worsening, always at the edge of catastrophe — such are things — the genius appears before his father not because of some circumstance, but despite circumstance. Following him there is no elevation of the family. He expends himself, and what's left behind is quickly spent as well. If his memory is held at all, it's either in curious regard as if he were a novel species of insect, or in outright contempt like any other insect. His work requires him to unmake himself. After it's done, there is only the slow, declining tendency which preceded him. Of course. Lone study can lead nowhere else. So Atlantis sank, so Alexandria burned.

Once the rational automaton regards itself, it will never again regard anything else. Like a mirror facing a mirror. For the logical positivist there is a similar sense: the infinite abyss, and yet, at the same time, a total lack of depth. Whether he can tell or not, his worldview is entirely contained within the aphorism: That which is articulable, is, and that which is inarticulable, is not.

Perhaps the world only turns on account of the multitude of dead looking on and rolling endlessly in their graves.

Over the years we've managed to retain some measure of sympathy for those who wish it all were not so, so to speak. Romantic as that sort of thing is. But for those who believe it doesn't have to be, no — as Yeats wrote, with age we *"wither away into the truth."* No, for them, anything beyond scorn would be a charity.

Custom has rarely made the struggle of great men seem noble at the time.

How insidious it is, putting your well-being on being well liked.

Vanity is a fine motivating force, if even a humane one, so long as the ox isn't left to trample the field.

Most forms of mundane mental illness or commonly diagnosed psychosis are only those behaviors that result when a man never manages to escape polite company for long enough to take himself seriously. Therapists, then, exist to *intellectualize* the unnatural, to dress it in laboratory language. They serve to convince such a person that the inhumane environment in which he finds himself is, at the root, his own fault, that it is a consequence of his personal perspective, a thing of his own making — and, of course, to profit off the continual maintenance of that delusion.

Give a man a decision and he will choose poorly. Make the right decision for him, and he will resent you for it. No one is master of anything who does not understand this principle.

On the accusation of being too judgmental: If you're not able to see the fault in someone else, how on earth do you expect to be able to exorcise it in yourself?

Nobody likes someone who writes like he's trying to convince himself.

What could be more diabolical than revealing to a person what it is that others avoid in him — because no one can avoid himself. Not once he knows.

For man after industry, the ideal comes first, and the labor lies in forcing the world to adhere to it. We could call this approach 'from the top-down,' in the sense that it begins with a conclusion and, arranges things so as to suit it. For man of antiquity, however, the labor came first. In time, and through conflict between body and mentality, the nature of the world is slowly revealed. We could call this approach 'from the bottom-up' in the opposing sense, that conclusions are drawn from things as they are, according to the terms which best represent them. The former legislates compliance, while the latter mythologized discipline.

One cannot work in such a way that no one else has to work, and one cannot suffer in such a way that no one else has to suffer.

The essence of masculinity is not the absence of emotion, but mastery over emotion. Both appear stoic, but only one is a man — the other is wearing a costume.

The vast majority of literature on the subject of the symbolic arts is completely useless; either desperate to sound intelligent at the expense of substance, or so far off the rails that any substantial conclusion is precluded entirely by stylistic mania. What we can say for certain is that any man of antiquity who took magical matters seriously would have been as disgusted with the state of things now as we are.

Alchemy is not, as is often supposed, a "primitive" science. In fact, the near opposite is true. Science is alchemy stripped of the humanities. It is epistemology, which connects the arts to the sciences. In the chivalric tradition, for example, alchemy *is* that specific epistemology.

Modern man sees nothing but coercion in posterity, because he reduces becoming to a manner of being. The grail eludes him.

We hate what is given, but love what is taken. So young men hate their lots, and old men care for their legacies.

Why is it that those who lack the constitution for the polemic are always so effete? Probably for the same reason that those who demand equity are always so measly. Polemicist and poet are brothers.

Perhaps that's what makes you a good man — knowing when to stop.

Whether or not you were right, being the difference between presumption and clairvoyance.

Hyperclassicism let them call it who suffer from the need to name something in order to have a neck around which to hang a placard of accusations. But understand, despite what is said in the tribunals, that in truth they only accuse themselves and allege, in so many words, exclusively the crime of humanity.

All legacy suffers either oblivion or molestation.

For our part, we have no interest in sitting under the sword. The political problem can be summarized for the sake of the point at hand: One person harbors the want for power over others, and as a result, he is predisposed to corruption. Another *lacks* the want for power over others, and therefore resists corruption. No system of governance can be devised for the purpose of luring the second person to power, because it's against his nature. No matter how you dress it up, he does not value holding power over anyone but himself. That is why you want him. If he were different, he would be the first sort of person. Therefore, every system of political authority can only hope to be configured so as to mitigate the inevitable corruption of the nefarious sort who have any interest in being there at all. So, one may recognize on reflection that we are less concerned with political ideals, and more concerned with political *limitations* in practice. Burke noted as much, after Robespierre and his tribunals laid waste to Paris. Of course, he was right. The entire Western world still suffers from having been afflicted with that "revolutionary" nescience, though we are taught to call it flattering things and conflate it with technological improvements to our quality of life. In light of this, we would only advance, as far as our own political convictions, that giving more bureaucrats more latitude does not have the effect of limiting corruption. It has the opposite effect. We are wary of any government that is not sufficiently wary of itself.

What more proof do we need that our so-called "democratic elections" are a fraud, than that the ballots are proprietary technology?

It's true that a crown doesn't make a king, but then, what sort of king has no crown?

There is an excellent remark in Heinlein about the 'beautiful poetry' of the American Constitution. Something of the usefulness of rights could be appended — to the effect that rights are only what civilities men can retain for themselves when challenged. Similarly, one of the Marxist's favorite fictions is the idea that private property either shouldn't, or *doesn't* exist. The response is equally hilarious: I have this thing, and you cannot take it away from me. Therefore it's my property whether you like it or not. Having said as much in 'educated' company, one will have to duck impotent tomatoes. So it is with rights. Gone are the days of the duel, with which none of this would have transpired.

So much talk of moderates and centrists. What is a moderate? Another fashion of conclusive terror, synthesis by an antiseptic name. A moderate is one who would hand over his heart or his spine if it meant he'd be *allowed* to keep the other.

128

The people will always endure subjugation, because compulsion *defines* the people. This is the only satisfactory explanation for the desperation with which the public seeks out its own enthrallment; which is to say, no explanation at all — such is their nature, and explanations may follow on from there.

A good liar does not tell lies so much as he reconfigures his own understanding of what is true.

Whoever convinced us that Galileo's prosecutors were men of the cloth, and not fat, hylic bureaucrats dressed in the cloth, ought to have been shot.

Ehrmann famously writes in his *Desiderata*: "No doubt the universe is unfolding as it should." Saying as much will provoke protest from a principled man. He will argue, no, just because something is given to happen doesn't make it right. But that's the problem. We put it to him that what's right is by nature that which is given to occur. Rightness, then, arises from an element of natural tendency. What he means when he says "right," and what right is, are two different things. He attempts, knowingly or unknowingly, to offer a definition of art as an ontological point. He says "right," but he means "ought." What ought is manmade, is man himself inasmuch as man is defined by what he makes, and what he does not. What *ought*, then, is a question of justice, and justice, though aesthetic and desirable, is nevertheless only aligned with that natural tendency as a matter of circumstance. When those things chance to align, we call the result artful. When they do not, we call it injustice.

So many moderns are in the business of quietly creating a problem to then solve loudly, and at great expense.

The man who in antiquity would have been a priest to a corrupt orthodoxy is today a committee-member, a bureaucrat, a politician's assistant, or an academic at some university. Yesterday he played with his scales and cuttings of coins, today he fiddles with his lists and his tables just the same. He shuffles things around to reflect the will of the funding, and jockeys for the approval of the fellows who feed him and who keep him fat. So it is with the intellectuals.

Scientists are the envy of all Puritans, and the greatest of all Protestants.

How annoying it is to be told what you must believe. It's significantly worse than being told what you must do.

History has demonstrated time and again that the real magic of the secular state is the ability of its party-men to call for power, and the willingness of its serfs to bloody their hands among each other in order to render it to them.

Revolution: A grotesque portrait of entropy.

While it may appear that politics is a game of words and money, in reality money can be repossessed and devalued, and words can be repurposed, re-interpreted, stifled, or esteemed — through violence. Civility is an emergent quality of armistice. That is, civility is defined in terms of violence; on the threat of physical compliance are founded all the more complex and polite manners of civil authority, and of non-violent methods of control. War is politics unalloyed.

Before the gates of the nation in its death throes one will always find the rotting heads of the priest-caste, speared and spitted, and flying on the crenellations above in a southerly wind, three standards: Positivism, Dialectic, and Soteriology.

More than they wish to be ruled, most men wish not to know it.

The real issue is whether or not the resolution of surveillance technologies is high enough to monitor people at so minuscule a scale, and so represent the ability to identify and disperse them. If it is, then so long as its infrastructure remains in place, the home and whatever individual sovereignty it represents is impossible. If it is not, then the dissenting force will swell and, one way or another, reassert itself.

Clarity is the magic of the commoner, and short-sightedness his undoing.

What is occurring now is nothing but the end of a cycle of civilization. There is no way out. It cannot be that sort of question. Our grandfathers saw the apocalypse and were stricken. Our fathers were born into a nation on its knees, and we are born into a nation prostrate. Our sons will be flung ruthlessly into life with hardly the time to steal a single, strangled breath before the nation is shoveled over on them. There is no more reversing the positivistic corrosion in this place than there is talking a stone back up a hill, or legislating a tumor out of the brain. Entropy cannot be defeated, it is defeat *itself*. We are here to live out the end, or to die in opposition to it. The god of those who die is Hector, and the god of those who survive is Aeneas. So long as we survive, our lot is witness. Our struggle is chronicle. It is to disallow the use of our demise as a political tool for the slavers of the coming ages, who would twist myth into doctrine, make martyrs out of heroes, and who would distort the past in service of the present. Mark our graves with a quill and calipers.

If, when we meet him in Hell, the anonymous Christian fellow responsible for authoring *De Sublimitate* will agree not to criticize our writing overmuch, we will be happy to extend him the same courtesy.

* * *

Printed in the USA
CPSIA information can be obtained
at www.ICGtesting.com
LVHW010522011224
798027LV00003B/649